Reclaiming the Counter-Cultural Fierceness of the Early Church — Why the Modern Church Must Be Hated for the Right Reasons

IMPIOUS GALILEANS

MIKE BROCK

ISBN Number
979-8-89571-165-1 (paperback)
979-8-89571-166-8 (Ebook)
979-8-89571-167-5 (Hardcover)
979-8-89571-168-2 (Audiobook)

Book Design, Editing & Print by **Travis Howland**
www.thetippshop.com

DEDICATION

While these pages may chart my observations over the last two decades, I certainly didn't navigate that path alone. The path of ministry is a wild and demanding adventure, but it's one we have joyfully chosen for a lifetime. The profound joy in that calling, every breakthrough, and every victory that has truly mattered, is credited to my wife and partner, Ashley.

She is the one who could miraculously turn scarcity into abundance when resources were lean. She has been the steady heart of our family, the grace that held us all together when the pressure felt overwhelming or my own strength faltered. In every season, she has been the voice reminding me of our purpose, and her faith in God's promises has been the unshakable foundation for it all. She is my anchor and my joy, the reason I have any balance today—a truth that anyone who truly knows us can celebrate.

And to my children—Crew, Olive, and Pippa: You have journeyed alongside me through it all, seeing me at my best and my worst. My deepest hope is that you've seen a father, fueled by your love, constantly striving to better honor you and our Heavenly Father. I love you so very much. You are my heart.

ENDORSEMENTS

The Impious Galileans *explores the transformative principles that once changed the world through the early church's fierce love, radical generosity, and unwavering commitments. This book challenges modern readers to reignite a movement that can transform lives and communities today. Highly recommend for anyone longing to see the church thrive as a world-changing force once more!*

Peter Greer, President & CEO, HOPE International and coauthor Lead with Prayer

In a world of bigger and better, Mike Brock's introduction of an historic era's manifestation of Jesus Followers demands a reexamination of our modern metrics for the evaluation of church and what makes us meaningful in the eyes of God... This is no formula; rather, it's a framework for restoring the leverage possible when truth is activated by Spirit-driven believers who are institution weary but inspiration energized!

Bob Shank, Founder, The Master's Program

In an age where the Church often seeks relevance through conformity, The Impious Galileans is a prophetic call to return to the fierce, sacrificial love of the early Church. Mike Brock challenges us to embrace a Gospel that disrupts, re-stores, and prioritizes the marginalized. This book is a blue-print for a vibrant, mission-driven Church that lives the truth with conviction and grace.

Rob Hoskins, President, OneHope (former Oral Roberts University Chairman)

*In his outstanding book **The Impious Galileans**, Mike Brock shows us the way forward by looking back. Whether you are part of a house church or a mega church, the principles inside can help you be a force for the kingdom in your city. Anyone can point out the problem, but Mike has pointed to solutions which bring a vibrant hope for the future of the church in our day.*

Pastor Ken Foreman, Senior Pastor, Cathedral of Faith, cathedraloffaith.org

A call to action for the modern Church. It laments a shift from its vibrant, Spirit-led origins—marked by presence, radical love, and supernatural transformation—towards a focus on performance, programs, and metrics. Mike Brock argues that in this pursuit of relevance and excellence, the Church has risked losing its authenticity and its focus on the marginalized, the very people Jesus came for. It's a plea to return to the simplicity and raw power of the early Church: a faith driven by surrender, compassion, and a willingness to step into pain out of love, not for show. The message is a remind-er that true impact comes from the Spirit, not from strategy or noise. This is a timely and urgent message for any community seeking to rediscover its pur-pose and power.

Pastor Mike Servello, Founder & CEO at Compassion Coalition

FOREWORD

In my village, an ancient church has been converted into countryside flats. The stonework still echoes the beauty that the original architects envisioned, but when I pass by, I imagine the worship, fellowship, and teaching that once filled its nave. Now the windows glow with domestic life, and I wonder what it felt like on that final evening when the last congregant turned the key and left the sanctuary in silence. The image poses a question to every living church.

The late Tim Keller of Redeemer Presbyterian Church in Manhattan put it starkly: *"If you and your church were to disappear off the face of the earth tomorrow, would anyone in the community around you notice you were gone? ... would they say 'we are really glad they are gone,' or 'we are really going to miss them'?"*

That question reflects a sobering reality we see in all of our towns and villages. Gallup reports that only about three in ten U.S. adults now attend religious services weekly or almost weekly—evidence of long-term decline and increasing secularism. Simultaneously, research compiling Barna's findings shows pastors struggling under the burden of ministry, with a third considering quitting and significant drops in well-being across various measures. Busyness and larger programmes alone have not translated into health, credibility, or fruit.

And yet, in the cracks of our moment, green shoots are pushing through. Across cities and campuses in Europe, the UK, and US, there is renewed interest in historic Christian faith—a longing for roots, ritual, and strong communities of belonging that can endure amid cultural upheaval. People are not chasing novelty; they are seeking substance - worship that shapes reality, a people whose love is tangible, and a mission that transcends the news cycle.

That is why Mike Brock's *The Impious Galileans* serves as a timely call. The title borrows Emperor Julian's sharp label for the early Christians 'impious' because they refused to burn incense to the gods, "Galileans" because they centered their lives on Jesus of Nazareth. Julian reluctantly recognized what he could not replicate: Christians outshone the empire, feeding not only their own poor but also those of the empire. Policy could not rival a people whose charity grew from worship and whose hope was grounded in a different economy. Brock does not long for a bygone golden age; he calls us to rediscover the practices that made the earliest communities so strangely captivating—radical generosity, all-member witness, disciplined prayer and fasting, and a practical holiness that was both countercultural and irresistibly humane.

Read this book, then, not as a quick "how-to," but as a clarion call to become a certain kind of people. The small group study guide will help you get started and the transformation begins where the early church did: at the Lord's table, in shared life, and through the Spirit's power. With repentance and worship that focus on Jesus; disciplines that reshape our love; table fellowship that erases loneliness; mercy that invests itself in neighbors; and witness that belongs to everyone; the Kingdom of God comes to earth. The first believers were sometimes hated for the right reasons: they exposed idols by the radiance of God's love, and they would not submit to the empire's gods. May that be true of us.

When I pass that converted church, I do not pray for stone to become sacred again, but for people to be set ablaze again - so that if, God forbid, our doors ever did close, our towns would feel the loss in hospitals and schools, on high streets and in homes, in griefs shared and meals served. May the Spirit make us such a people; may this book steady our hands for the work; and may our communities someday say, "We would sorely miss them."

Donovan Palmer
CEO Mission Aviation Fellowship International [1]
(former CEO of Mercy Ships)

CONTENTS

Part III.
Reclaiming the Galilean Spirit – A Path Forward for a World-Transforming Movement

Part IV.
Confronting Modern Crises with Galilean Compassion

Part V.
The Fierce Future – A Counter-Cultural Movement Once More

PREFACE

This book was written from a place of deep conviction, born out of a Christology that sees the Church as the central and beloved place for Christ's glorious return. It is offered not as another voice tearing down, taking shots, or attempting to expose the Bride of Christ. Its purpose is the opposite. This work is intended as a blueprint for protection, an appeal to build and uplift, and a vision for how the Church can, and must, be its absolute best. This work is for those who are frustrated, yet relentlessly optimistic.

For the young pastor, standing at the trailhead of a long and daunting ministry, trying to make sense of the journey ahead, feeling the weight of expectation and the confusion of a landscape that seminary classes never fully prepared them for. The prayer is that these pages offer not only a map but also a deep and abiding hope for the path God has called them to walk.

For the faithful congregant, devout elder the lifelong member who sits in the chairs and feels a quiet, persistent sense that the church has lost its way. For those who remember a time of greater fire, of simpler devotion, of more tangible impact, and long to see it again, this book is an affirmation that they are not alone in that feeling, and that there is a path to return to our first love.

For the committed steward who faithfully gives their 10% tithe but whose heart yearns to do so much more. For those who look at the world's immense needs and the Church's incredible potential, and who are ready to unleash a flood of generosity—if only they could see a ministry wholly committed to transforming communities. This book is an earnest attempt to paint a picture of that very church, a church so effective and so alive that it compels and justifies radical, openhanded giving.

For the faith-based non-profit leader, out on the front lines doing the hard and holy work of ministry in the streets, the shelters, and the broken places of our world. For those who love the Church, yet often feel disenfranchised and on their own, wishing that the institution they serve would truly see them, feeling abandoned by its deviation from the very mission they are sacrificing to fulfill. This book is a call for that reunion, a case for the local church to once again become the champion and engine of the transformative work they do every day.

For the pastor who began because they heard the calling but now feels caught up in the relentless machinery of management—property, team building, organizational issues, loans, and HR. For those whose time feels consumed not by pastoral care, but by property concerns; not by discipleship, but by debt. For those who began the journey to shepherd souls, but now feel more like a COO, and just want to return to simpler times, this work presents a challenge: reclaim the impious Galilean stand. This book is a permission slip to re-center ministry on the fierce, simple, and people-focused mission that first captured the heart.

And finally, this book is an invitation for those who felt "done" with the church—the deconstructionist, the burned out, the hurt, and the miffed. It's for those who, despite their frustrations, still hold a love for the church and a belief in its divine calling. As the world grows more challenging and culture becomes darker and more complex, it's precisely when the spirit of the "Impious Galilean" shines brightest. This is a call to journey back to our fierce, counter-cultural, and irresistibly compassionate roots, and together, create a groundswell of faith worth building again.

It is essential that this journey be undertaken with grace and mercy. This is not a call to judgment or to the sin of comparison, pitting one church model against another. From the vibrant intimacy of a home church to the broad reach of a mega-church, every expression of the Body of Christ has its vital place and purpose. This is, instead, an invitation for each of us to listen to our own personal nudge from the Holy Spirit—to feel that internal conviction to want the Impious Galilean way for ourselves, in our own hearts and contexts.

INTRODUCTION: THE MODERN CHURCH'S DILEMMA AND AN ANCIENT INVITATION

The modern church stands at a crossroads. A quiet but persistent unease, felt across the theological spectrum, suggests we've lost our way. Symptoms abound: declining engagement, a "silent exodus" of younger generations, and a missional vision that too often feels muted, institutional, and inwardly focused. We pour immense energy and resources into maintaining our structures, yet we struggle to make a truly transformative impact on the world around us. This begs a crucial question: How can the church reclaim the fierce, counter-cultural, and world-changing identity that defined its earliest days?

This book contends the answer isn't found in a new program or modern innovation, but by drawing inspiration from an unexpected historical source: the early Christians of Galilee. The Roman Emperor Julian the Apostate derisively labeled them "impious Galileans"—a moniker we intentionally re-appropriate as a badge of honor. This term symbolizes a commitment to radical, counter-cultural practices that fundamentally challenged the established imperial religious and social order of their time.

Why "Impious Galileans"? A Historical Validation

To be clear, this book is not an exercise in deconstruction or an indictment of the Church. I deeply love the Church—the Bride of Christ—and my earnest desire is to see it thrive, flourish, and reclaim its profound world-transforming impact. My critical examination of contemporary challenges stems from a deep hope and conviction that the Church can, and must, embody its ancient, fierce, and compassionate call once more. Furthermore, my focus on certain institutional challenges, such as financial models, should in no way be interpreted as a blanket condemnation of all types of churches. I recognize that every expression of the Body of Christ, from intimate house church gatherings to sprawling mega-churches and everything in between, has its vital place and purpose. My aim is to foster discernment and encourage a return to foundational principles that can strengthen all expressions of the Church, for its crucial role in the world today.

The reputation of the early church wasn't manufactured; it was forged by the radical character and actions of its people. Julian the Apostate, who reigned from 361 to 363 CE, embarked on a determined mission to reverse the Christianization of the Roman Empire and restore traditional pagan practices. Educated in the classical traditions, Julian deemed Christianity intellectually and morally deficient. Instead of widespread persecution, he used calculated political and social strategies to undermine Christian influence. These included revoking privileges, restoring pagan temples, and prohibiting Christians from teaching classical literature—a move designed to sever their access to cultural influence and marginalize them from public life. His derogatory label, "impious Galileans," was a deliberate attempt to dismiss and demean Christians. [2]

Yet, despite his hostility, Julian inadvertently provided compelling external validation of early Christian distinctiveness: their radical, universal charity. He lamented, "For it is a disgrace... that the impious Galileans feed our people in addition to their own, whereas ours manifestly lack assistance from us."[2] This statement from an adversary powerfully attests to the effectiveness of Christian benevolence. Julian even attempted to force pagan priests to imitate Christian charity, ordering the establishment of hostels and distributing state subsidies for the poor. However, this imitation was fundamentally flawed, "doomed to failure from the start because it was artificial." [3] The pagan worldview lacked the theological framework to support genuine care for the poor, often viewing them as inferior. This historical failure teaches a critical lesson: true, sustainable, and impactful benevolence isn't merely a pragmatic policy; it's the natural outcome of deeply held theological conviction. The "supernatural value" of Christian charity arose from an internal, spiritual motivation, not external compulsion. If the modern church seeks to increase its charitable impact, it must first re-examine and re-cultivate the underlying spiritual motivations that produce such radical generosity, rather not simply adjusting budgets or implementing new programs without internal transformation.

Our Journey Ahead

This book will journey through history, examining the authentic behaviors, character, and disciplines that defined the early Christians, particularly those from Galilee. We will draw clear comparisons and contrasts with the contemporary evangelical church, providing a well-researched, compelling, and practical guide for rediscovery and transformative action.

Next, we will hold up a mirror to the modern church, critically examining the "internal gravitation" that pulls our resources and attention inward. We will diagnose how this leads to bloated budgets that minimize mission, small groups that suffer from "missional drift," and a struggle to disciple people away from the cultural allure of the world.

But this book does not stop at diagnosis. The heart of our journey is to chart a practical and hopeful path forward.

We will explore concrete strategies for a profound financial reformation that prioritizes the greater community that surrounds us and unleashes generosity. We will outline how to revitalize evangelism by shifting from a solo approach to a communal a calling. We will make the case for restoring the full, five-fold ministry leadership of apostles, prophets, and evangelists alongside pastors and teachers, and we will champion the "ministry of all," empowering every believer to be a minister in their daily vocation.

Finally, we will see how this reclaimed Galilean spirit equips the church to be a credible, healing force in a world wracked by crises of loneliness, mental health, abuse, and youth disaffiliation. We will argue that the ultimate goal is not to be liked, but to become a church that is "hated for the right reasons"—not for hypocrisy or irrelevance, but for prophetically challenging a broken world with the irresistible and counter-cultural love of Jesus Christ. This is a call to become a fierce movement once more.

PART 1

THE PORTRAIT OF A FIERCE MOVEMENT – THE ORIGINAL "IMPIOUS GALILEANS"

CHAPTER 1

JULIAN'S GAZE:
WHAT THE EMPEROR SAW (AND ENVIED)

Julian's reign was characterized by a deliberate effort to dismantle the Christian establishment and restore traditional paganism. He believed Christianity was a "corrupting influence in society" and sought to diminish the Church's power through legal and political measures rather than overt persecution. His policies included removing privileges granted to Christians by Constantine, reopening pagan temples, restoring temple lands, and notably, issuing an edict forbidding Christians from teaching classical literature, astutely designed to cut off Christians from a primary source of influence and undermine their social standing.

Born into the Constantinian dynasty, Julian was raised nominally Christian, but his early life was marred by the violence of the imperial court, including the massacre of many of his relatives by Christianized family members. This personal trauma, combined with his deep immersion in classical Greek philosophy, particularly Neo-Platonism, led him to vehemently reject Christianity. He found in Neo-Platonism a sophisticated intellectual and spiritual framework that offered a cosmic order, a rich pantheon of gods, and rituals that he believed embodied genuine piety and intellectual depth, far superior to the Christian faith he had been forced to adopt. [4]
For Julian, Christianity represented a departure from ancient

wisdom and civic virtue, leading to his passionate endeavor to restore what he perceived as the true, philosophical religion of the Roman Empire.

Despite his animosity, Julian's observations of Christians were remarkably astute, particularly concerning their social welfare efforts. He explicitly acknowledged the "kindness of Christians to strangers, their care for the burial of their dead, and the sobriety of their lifestyle". [5] What particularly astonished him was the Christians' universal benevolence, extending their charity not only to their own members but also to pagans, beggars, and strangers. This widespread, inclusive generosity was a striking feature that fundamentally distinguished them from other religious groups of the era.

Recognizing the social power and appeal of Christian charity, Julian, as Pontifex Maximus (high priest of paganism), initiated a program to compel pagan priests to emulate these Christian practices. He ordered the establishment of hostels in every city for strangers and mandated the distribution of state-subsidized grain and wine to the poor. However, this imitation was merely "a pragmatic move," devoid of genuine compassion. The fundamental flaw in Julian's plan was that the pagan worldview lacked the theological foundation for universal love and the intrinsic equality of all people; instead, it often viewed the poor as inferior. Consequently, Julian's artificial charity was "doomed to failure from the start".

The emperor's inability to replicate Christian charity, despite recognizing its profound societal impact, reveals a crucial truth: true, sustainable, and broadly impactful benevolence stems from a deep-seated worldview and theological conviction, not merely from policy, pragmatic strategy, or governmental subsidies. This historical failure serves as a critical cautionary tale for the modern church. It indicates that if you, as part of the modern church, seek to increase your charitable impact, you must first cultivate the spiritual and theological roots that inspire genuine, self-sacrificial giving, rather than simply reallocating budget lines or adopting new programs without internal transformation. The "supernatural value" inherent in Christian charity meant it did not require external subsidies, unlike Julian's forced program, thereby highlighting the intrinsic and deeply motivated nature of their generosity.

CHAPTER 2

LIFE IN ANCIENT GALILEE: SIMPLICITY, COMMUNITY, AND A PEOPLE-DRIVEN CHURCH

Life in Galilean villages during the time of Jesus (1st century AD) was characterized by modesty and simplicity. Homes were typically small, constructed from stacked fieldstones and mud, with packed-dirt floors, often clustered around shared courtyards. Luxury items were absent, furnishings were limited, and families generally lived at subsistence levels due to high taxes. The majority of inhabitants were hardworking farmers, fishermen, and artisans, whose daily lives were deeply intertwined with their extended families. Public buildings were minimal, frequently limited to synagogues that served as community centers and schools.

The earliest Christian communities, including those that emerged in Galilee, did not gather in grand edifices but convened in private homes or humble huts, known as "house churches". The Greek term *ekklesia*, from which the English word "church" is derived, literally meant "assembly," "gathering," or "congregation," emphasizing the collective body of believers rather than a physical building. These early gatherings were intimate, often urban and plebeian in character, involving communal activities such as singing hymns, reading scriptures, holding all-night prayer sessions, and sharing meals, including the Eucharist. As exemplified by the early followers in Jerusalem, they actively "shared their goods, and met one another's needs" (Acts 2:44-45, 4:32-35). The church, as an institution, did not make these early believers; rather, their radical commitment, shared life, and fervent faith forged the very reputation and identity of the church. The reputation of the church came directly from the reputation of its people.

As the early Christian movement expanded, practical needs within the community became increasingly apparent, especially the care for widows afflicted by poverty. To address these needs efficiently and ensure the equitable distribution of aid, the office of deacon was formally established, as described in Acts 6:1-6. This development demonstrates an early, structured, and intentional commitment to social welfare and mutual care within the embryonic church, with specific individuals designated to oversee these vital functions.

The organic growth of the early church varied approach, characterized by decentralized house churches and a plebeian, community-driven ethos, stands in stark contrast to the later institutionalization of Christianity in the 4th century. Christianity began as a movement centered around Jesus, a charismatic teacher, whose disciples were often ordinary people like fishermen and artisans. These early followers gathered in humble private homes, and the movement spread through personal relationships, social networks, and the fervent zeal of ordinary believers.

After Julian, Christianity became the official state religion of the Roman Empire. During this period, worship practices became "more elaborate," the distinction between laity and clergy "more pronounced," and worship spaces began to be "modeled on the basilica style". Even in Galilee, large cathedrals with dedicated baptismal halls were constructed. This evolution from a "marginal, persecuted, and popularly despised Christian sect" to a "fully institutionalized church capable of embracing the entire Roman empire" involved a significant transformation in structure and emphasis. While institutionalization provided stability and facilitated wider reach, it also led to a *corpus permixtum* (a mixed body), where sanctity increasingly resided in the institution itself rather than solely in the radical commitment of individual members. The contemporary concern about the modern church being "expensive to run" is not merely a recent phenomenon but a long-term consequence of this historical institutionalization, potentially leading to a diversion of resources from direct mission and charity to the maintenance of infrastructure and professional clergy.

Institutionalized, larger, or otherwise, are not bad; they simply come with different challenges. In fact the profound and often positive impact the Church has had on the world throughout history, in its institutionalized forms. Indeed, the Church, despite its flaws and challenges, has been a singular force for good in countless ways. For instance, monastic communities served as beacons of learning and social welfare, preserving ancient texts, developing agricultural innovations, and providing early forms of hospitals and care for the sick and poor. The Church was also a primary patron of the arts, inspiring masterpieces of painting, sculpture, architecture, and music that continue to enrich humanity. Furthermore, the foundations for the rise of modern science and higher education were often laid within Christian intellectual traditions and institutions, reflecting a belief in an ordered, knowable universe created by a rational God. Without the enduring influence of the medieval and later Church, our world's cultural, social, and intellectual landscape would undoubtedly look vastly different, a testament to its multifaceted (and often beneficial) impact, despite its many internal struggles and shortcomings.

CHAPTER 3

CORE CHARACTERISTICS: BEHAVIORS, CHARACTER, AND DISCIPLINES

Radical Generosity and Sacrificial Care

At the core of Jesus's message was the "proclamation of the coming Reign of God," which offered "good news to the poor". This message included a strong prophetic critique of wealth, with passages like Luke's Beatitudes pronouncing "Woe to you who are rich" and the story of the Rich Young Man illustrating a call to radical generosity and a rejection of material possessions, emphasizing that "one cannot... serve both God and Mammon". This established a foundational "option for the poor" as a core theological and ethical imperative for early believers. This radical open-handedness and commitment to works of service for the widow, the poor, the orphan, and the incarcerated was a defining mark of their faith, representing a return to true religion (James 1:27).

Early Christian communities actively pooled their economic resources. The letters of the Apostle Paul frequently discuss aid collected in Greece and Turkey for the "saints" in Jerusalem, explicitly stating its purpose was to "remember the poor". While local charity was common, a broader network of support emerged by the late second century. Groups like those in Rome began directing capital to non-local needs, assisting impoverished Christian communities in other cities (such as Corinth) and even those sent to mines due to persecution. This extensive support network was fostered by a strong sense of "siblingship" among believers.

Unlike Julian's cynical, pragmatic attempts to mimic Christian charity, the early church's generosity was rooted in a deep theological conviction. They firmly believed that acts of kindness and service to "the least ones" were done directly "for Christ" (Matthew 25:40), imbuing their charity with "supernatural value". This inherent motivation meant that true charity did not necessitate governmental subsidies or external coercion, but flowed freely and spontaneously from their faith. This spirit of giving, both corporately and individually, was a hallmark of their kindness and generosity.

For early Christians, radical generosity and comprehensive care for the poor were not optional programs or a small percentage of a budget, but a direct, non-negotiable expression of their core theology and Jesus's teachings. This stands in sharp contrast to the modern church's tendency to compartmentalize "benevolence" into a distinct, often minimal, budget category. Jesus's teachings explicitly centered on the poor and issued a profound critique of wealth. This was not a mere suggestion but a fundamental aspect of the "Reign of God" that he proclaimed. This theological foundation directly led to practical, radical actions within the early communities, including the communal sharing of goods, the establishment of deacons specifically for the care of the poor, and widespread, networked financial aid. Even an external, hostile observer like Julian recognized this pervasive and effective charity.

In the modern context, however, this foundational "option for the poor" often appears diminished in budgetary priorities. Indeed, multiple analyses of contemporary church finances reveal that a very small percentage of church funds directly reaches the materially poor or funds external missions. For example, a 2014 study by Christianity Today's Church Law &

Tax Group found that churches, on average, allocated around 1% of their budget specifically to 'benevolence' (direct aid to the poor). [8] While this figure highlights a significant area for potential growth in direct material support, it's also important for you to recognize that the Church's mission extends beyond purely financial assistance. The 'poor in spirit'—those struggling with anxiety, depression, loneliness, and relational brokenness—also represent a profound area of need that requires the church's compassionate attention, often through relational ministry, spiritual formation, and communal care. This book advocates for a holistic approach to generosity and service, one that prioritizes both tangible aid for the materially impoverished and comprehensive 'soul care' for those deeply wounded in spirit, reflecting the multifaceted compassion of the early 'impious Galileans'. More broadly, research from empty tomb, inc., [6] analyzing 2019 data, indicated that 84% of congregational income was spent on the church's internal activities, leaving approximately 16% for the 'larger mission of the church', which includes but is not limited to direct aid to the poor. These figures stand in stark contrast to the significant portions of church budgets consumed by staff salaries and facility costs, which together often account for 70-75% or more of total expenditures. This financial structure suggests a fundamental shift from the early church's model, where resources were pooled for immediate, direct needs of the poor and communal living was simpler. The modern church's budget appears primarily geared towards maintaining an organization and providing services to its members, rather than prioritizing radical external impact. Furthermore, the ambiguity in how 'charity' or 'missions' is reported can create a perception that more is being done externally than is actually the case, potentially hindering genuine self-assessment and reform.

Reclaiming the Galilean spirit means reintegrating the "option for the poor" as a theological driver for all financial decisions. Peter Greer, [7] reflecting on the motivations for serving the poor, powerfully echoes this sentiment: "We love because God first loved us (1 John 4:19)... When we truly understand the gift of grace we've been given in Christ, we just can't help ourselves from showing love to anyone hurting or in a desperate situation". He further emphasizes that service to others is "a testament to the Gospel," noting how difficult it is for people to "disagree with a life of service to others". Greer explicitly references Julian the Apostate's observations of early Christian charity, reinforcing the historical validity of their unique commitment to the poor and its undeniable impact on those outside the faith. This perspective aligns perfectly with the idea that radical generosity is not a mere budgetary line item, but a natural, compelled outflow of a heart transformed by God's grace.

Zealous Evangelism and Outward Focus

Early Christians were remarkably intentional in sharing the Gospel, often leveraging natural relationships for evangelistic opportunities. This included one-on-one conversations, such as Andrew bringing his brother Peter to Jesus, or Philip bringing Nathaniel, and strategic evangelism within households, where believing spouses served as witnesses to unbelieving ones, and children were raised "in the discipline and instruction of the Lord". Missions was not a separate department but an inherent part of life for every believer, extending kindness and generosity to both the unsaved and saved community, as well as those from other religions. The earliest church was also deeply committed to the public proclamation of the Gospel, with believers actively preaching in synagogues and marketplaces, as exemplified by Peter's sermon on Pentecost or Paul's reasoning in Athens. They also engaged in "apologetics," providing a "reasoned defense" of their faith and adapting their message to the cultural and intellectual contexts of their audiences.

A striking characteristic of early Christian evangelism was its pervasive, organic nature. Ordinary Christians, even those described by pagan critics like Celsus as "wool workers, cobblers, laundry workers and the most illiterate and bucolic yokels," actively "gossiped the Gospel" in their daily lives and workplaces. This demonstrated a "steady zeal" for mission, without the need for formal "mission societies" as understood today. The movement spread significantly through individual witness and established social networks.

The early church's evangelism was a pervasive, organic aspect of daily life for all believers, not primarily a specialized program or the sole responsibility of clergy. This contrasts with the modern church's tendency to compartmentalize evangelism into specific programs or events, often separate from daily life or relegated to a few "gifted" individuals. The events that often transpire are often focused on pushing for attendance on Easter, Christmas, or other significant holidays. Millions of dollars are spent around the country on Easter egg hunts, Halloween alternative events, and Christmas productions with little or no tangible evidence of church growth, salvations, or practical needs being met. The observation that the modern church spends "more time encouraging small groups and attendance than evangelism" is notable. Lifeway research indicates that less small group participation correlates with fewer new commitments to Christ. [9] While pastors express a high desire for members to engage in evangelism (85%), the practical emphasis may be different. The early church's evangelistic success stemmed from a culture where every believer understood their role as a witness. The challenge for the modern church is to move beyond simply having evangelism programs to fostering a missional culture where outward focus is inherent to the church's identity and every member's discipleship. If internal programs, such as small groups, do not effectively equip and propel members into outward mission, they risk becoming insular and failing to fulfill the Great Commission.

Disciplined Community and Spiritual Practices

Early Christians cultivated a strong reputation for distinct moral and communal discipline, a characteristic evident from both Christian and pagan sources. They practiced a tiered approach to confronting sin, as outlined in Matthew 18:15-17: starting with private admonition, then involving one or two witnesses, and finally presenting the matter to the broader church body, with the ultimate goal of restoration. Even pagan observers like Pliny the Younger noted Christians' vows to avoid wrongdoing. Their lives were marked by counter-culturalism and kindness, equipping them to be godly.

Core spiritual disciplines were deeply integrated into their daily lives and communal worship. These included memorizing Scripture, particularly the Psalms and Gospels, and singing and praying the Psalms. Regular prayer, such as praying the Lord's Prayer three times a day, and consistent fasting (typically on Wednesdays and Fridays, often until sundown with simple meals) were common practices, viewed as means of spiritual formation and self-denial. Weekly gatherings for communion, worship, and fellowship were fundamental and universally observed. A commitment to simplicity of life, often involving the willingness to give away possessions to the poor and needy (as seen in Acts 4) and living contentedly, was also a notable characteristic. This discipline extended beyond material possessions to attitudes, including avoiding drama, gossip, and striving for peaceful relations with others.

The early church's rigorous internal discipline and consistent spiritual practices were not merely personal piety but a collective commitment that made them distinct, credible, and compelling to outsiders, including Julian. This internal strength and coherence served as the wellspring from which their radical generosity and zealous evangelism flowed. Early Christians were characterized by specific, pervasive spiritual disciplines (prayer, fasting, scripture engagement) and a robust system of communal moral accountability. Julian himself noted their "sobriety of their lifestyle", and Pliny observed their vows to avoid wrongdoing. This internal character was visibly manifest externally. A community that lives out its values internally presents a more credible and attractive witness externally.

If the modern church perceives itself as having "lost its way" in terms of external impact (evidenced by low charity and less evangelism), a root cause may lie in a weakening of these foundational internal disciplines and communal accountability. Reclaiming the "impious Galilean" identity therefore necessitates a renewed commitment to these often-unseen, fundamental practices that shape individual and communal character, recognizing that internal vitality is a prerequisite for sustained external influence. Peter Greer warns against "the spiritual danger of doing good" when service becomes about self-promotion also underscore the need for deep personal and communal spiritual disciplines to maintain right motives. "Our service is downstream from the Gospel message. Simply, it's a response to God's generosity". This emphasizes that the outward flow of generosity and service must come from a deep internal wellspring of spiritual formation and gratitude, rooted in rigorous and intentional spiritual practices.

CHAPTER 4

FAITH AND PHILANTHROPY IN A PAGAN EMPIRE: WOMEN, ORPHANS, AND THE GALILEAN SPIRIT UNDER JULIAN

Introduction: The Church Endures in a Shifting Empire

The 4th century AD was a period of significant change for the Roman Empire and the booming Christian faith. The reign of Flavius Claudius Julianus, Julian the Apostate continued to marginalize and silence the Galileans. In this environment of shifting religious and political landscapes, the early Christian communities continued to live out their faith, often in ways that starkly contrasted with the surrounding culture. This chapter explores two key aspects of their witness during this era: the vital roles played by women within the church and the deep commitment to caring for orphans – both powerful reflections of the enduring "Impious Galilean" spirit of radical love and compassion.

The Evolving Roles of Women in the 4th Century Church:

While societal norms of the Roman Empire, including in its eastern provinces, often relegated women to domestic roles and limited public influence, the Christian church provided a space where women could actively participate in ministry and service. This was rooted in a theology where, in Christ, there is "neither Jew nor Gentile, neither slave nor free, nor is there male and female, for you are all one in Christ Jesus" (Galatians 3:28). By the 4th century, the roles of women in the church had evolved since the earliest days of Jesus' ministry in Galilee. The office of deaconess remained significant, with these women undertaking crucial tasks such as visiting the sick, ministering to the poor, assisting with baptisms (particularly of other women), and even providing instruction in Christian living. Writings from the period highlight the respect and importance accorded to deaconesses within their communities. Figures like Olympias, a wealthy and influential deaconess in Constantinople and a friend of John Chrysostom, exemplify the impactful service women provided.

Beyond the formal role of deaconess, many women, particularly widows, held respected positions within the church. Free from the traditional expectations of Roman patriarchy that often required remarriage, these women could dedicate themselves to prayer, service, and teaching other women. The church often provided financial support for enrolled widows, and in return, they contributed significantly to the spiritual and practical well-being of the community. These women weren't merely recipients of charity; they were active agents of it within the church. They often faced loneliness and marginalization in the broader society, and the church provided a vital sense of belonging and purpose. Their commitment to the poor and "poor in spirit" within their own communities was often profound.

It is important to note that theological debates regarding the roles of women were also emerging during this period. Influential thinkers began to articulate views that emphasized female subordination based on certain interpretations of scripture and prevailing philosophical ideas. Councils like the Synod of Laodicea (around 360 AD) even placed restrictions on women's roles, reflecting a tension that would continue to shape the church. However, alongside these developments, the active participation of women in various forms of ministry persisted, demonstrating their continued importance to the life and growth of the church. The existence of "presbyteresses" in some communities, while debated and eventually suppressed in many areas, further underscores the active leadership roles some women held. Many of these women, though playing vital roles, faced marginalization even within the church structure itself, highlighting an ongoing struggle for recognition.

Orphan Care as a Hallmark of Christian Practice:

The commitment to caring for the vulnerable, including orphans, was a deeply ingrained aspect of Christian faith and practice from its earliest days. By the 4th century, this commitment had manifested in more organized ways. While individual acts of charity within families and communities undoubtedly continued, the church increasingly took on a more formal role in providing for orphaned children. The establishment of orphanages, though perhaps not yet in the fully developed form they would take in later centuries, began during this period as Christian communities sought to live out the biblical mandate to care for the fatherless (James 1:27). In a world where abandoned children often faced dire circumstances, this proactive care demonstrated a radical commitment to those on the margins of society.

A particularly notable example of this commitment is the work of St. Basil the Great in the latter half of the 4th century. [4] In Caesarea (modern-day Turkey, but within the sphere of early church influence), Basil established the Basiliad, a comprehensive charitable complex that included facilities for the poor, the sick, and also orphans. This pioneering institution provided not just shelter and sustenance but also education, vocational training, and medical care, showcasing a holistic approach to caring for vulnerable children. While Basil himself was a key figure, it is highly likely that women within his community, potentially including deaconesses and dedicated female staff, played crucial roles in the daily care and nurturing of the orphans within the Basiliad. The dedication and practical support needed for such an endeavor would have undoubtedly involved the significant contributions of women, many of whom may have been immigrants or from marginalized communities themselves, driven by a deep empathy for those in need.

Christian Charity: A Light in a Pagan World:

The commitment of the 4th-century church to acts of charity extended far beyond just orphan care. Christians were known for their broad-based compassion, providing aid to the poor, the sick, the elderly, prisoners, and even strangers. This comprehensive approach to caring for the needy drew the attention of even their detractors. Julian the Apostate recognized that this selfless service was a powerful draw for people and contributed to the growth of the Christian faith. This highlights how the "Impious Galilean" spirit of radical love continued to shine brightly through their actions of mercy, reaching out to the lonely and those considered outcasts by wider society.

A Call to Modernity: Embracing the Full Power of Women in the Church:

The example of the 4th-century church, with its active involvement of women in service, teaching, and care for the vulnerable, serves as a powerful reminder for the modern church. While historical contexts and specific roles may evolve, the underlying principle of valuing and empowering the gifts and contributions of all believers, both men and women, remains foundational to the true essence of the "Galilean movement." Just as women played crucial roles in the early church – from supporting Jesus' ministry to caring for orphans and the poor – their active participation and leadership are vital for the health, vibrancy, and effectiveness of the church today. We must remember that the "poor in spirit," the lonely, the marginalized, and immigrants are all part of our communities and deserve to be embraced and valued within the church.

Sadly, even in contemporary settings, instances of marginalization of women's talents and callings within the church still occur. This not only limits the potential of individual women but also diminishes the overall strength and impact of the Christian community. [10] The spirit of the early church, and indeed the teachings of Jesus himself, call for a recognition of the inherent worth and diverse gifts that both men and women bring to the body of Christ. To truly embody the counter-cultural "fierceness" of the early Galileans, the modern church must actively work to dismantle any barriers that prevent women from fully serving and leading according to their God-given abilities. This includes actively seeking out and valuing the contributions of those who might feel lonely or marginalized within the congregation, as well as extending welcome and support to immigrants. Only then can the church truly reflect the inclusive and transformative love that characterized its earliest adherents.

PART 2

THE MODERN CHURCH TODAY – A CRITICAL EXAMINATION

CHAPTER 5

THE INTERNAL GRAVITATION: ATTENDANCE, SMALL GROUPS, AND MISSIONAL DRIFT

Church membership and regular attendance are experiencing a concerning decline across the U.S.. Fewer than half of U.S. adults now belong to a church, and approximately 4 in 10 no longer regularly attend religious services. This trend is particularly pronounced among younger generations: only 16% of Millennials and 15% of Gen Z consider church attendance important or attend regularly, significantly lower than older cohorts. This demographic shift indicates a growing disconnect from traditional institutional religion.

While small groups are widely adopted and often viewed as crucial for church growth and spiritual development, the average participation rate in Protestant churches is 44%, representing a decline from 49% in 2010. Critically, research indicates a correlation: "As we see less participation in groups, it is not surprising that churches see fewer people coming to Christ". This suggests that while small groups are intended for "building up" members and discipleship, they may not be effectively translating into outward evangelism and new conversions.

To be clear, the small group model was conceived and designed by Christ Himself—a small band of disciples called to go and do. They can be a profound source of community and spiritual growth. However, without this intentional missional design, they can inadvertently become part of the internal gravitation problem. Too often, they can evolve into exclusive clubs for established friends, silos for key church leaders, or "closed groups" where members are unwilling to disrupt the existing dynamic to welcome newcomers. Many are also formed around shared interests or life stages, which, while beneficial, can fail to create a place for the poor or the 'poor in spirit,' whose only shared commonality with other members might be a desperate desire for Jesus.

I remember taking my family to a new church after ten years of pastoring. We were so happy to be there and eagerly went through the suggested new member class. For three Sundays, we gathered in a back room, welcomed with freshly baked, amazing cookies and warm conversation. We were truly grateful for the effort and the desire to help us connect. The challenge came when we were told to find a small group. We saw several established groups of friends who were clearly already deeply connected. Though everyone was kind, it was difficult to find a place to land, as most of the groups felt closed. As a family that didn't fit neatly into one of the existing categories, we watched as most of the other new people also struggled to connect and eventually drifted away.

This experience, despite the church's genuine hospitality, highlights a critical point. When the primary—and often only— pathway to community is through small groups, we create unintentional barriers. By contrast, serving the community on mission together is naturally age-diverse and open to everyone; it builds powerful affinity and connection through a shared purpose. Small groups are great, but they cannot be the sole focus or modality for growth and community. If our main strategy for connection filters out the very people we are called to reach, perhaps a new model is needed.

When examining engagement in community service, evangelical pastors are less likely than mainline pastors to report a large percentage of adult participation. Only 9% of evangelical pastors report that 60% or more adults in their church volunteer in community service, compared to 15% for mainline pastors. This statistic suggests a potential de-emphasis on direct, hands-on community engagement within the evangelical context compared to other Christian traditions.

There exists an inherent and often debated tension within the church regarding its primary focus: should it be external (bringing new people in, evangelism) or internal (building up existing members, discipleship)? While both are essential for fulfilling the mission to "make disciples," an overemphasis on internal building without a clear, intentional outward thrust can lead to an insular community. This internal focus, intended to foster deep discipleship, faces a critical challenge when examining its actual outcomes. Recent worldview studies reveal a startling gap between affiliation and belief. According to Barna's research, a mere 6% of evangelicals and only 11% of those classified as "born again" actually possess a biblical worldview. [11] This suggests that even when the church succeeds at gathering people for internal programs, it is largely failing to instill the foundational convictions that shape a counter-cultural life, sometimes fostering what has been described as "fat sheep who fail to reproduce" or a "spirit of superiority".

Pastors' stated priorities often reflect this tension, with worship (29%) and teaching (27%) being top priorities, while evangelism is a desired outcome for members (85%) but not always a primary programmatic focus. The contemporary emphasis on small groups and attendance, while valuable for internal community and spiritual growth, risks becoming an end in itself if it does not intentionally and effectively translate into outward evangelism and tangible community service. This can lead to a "FUBU mentality" (for us by us) where the church becomes a comfortable club for existing members rather than a dynamic, missional force in the world.

The observation that the modern church spends "more time encouraging small groups and attendance than evangelism and community services" is a central point of concern for you to consider. This is supported by data indicating declining small group participation, which correlates with fewer new commitments to Christ. Additionally, evangelical pastors report lower community service participation compared to mainline counterparts. While pastors articulate a desire for members to engage in evangelism and helping the poor, their primary focus areas, such as worship and teaching, are often internally oriented. If discipleship within small groups is not explicitly equipping and motivating members for external mission, it can inadvertently contribute to an insular community. The declining attendance, particularly among younger generations, might be a symptom of a church perceived as internally focused and less relevant to the pressing needs and questions of the outside world. The "impious Galileans" were distinct precisely because they engaged the world with their radical faith, not retreated from it. The transformation requires a conscious effort to integrate mission into every aspect of church life and individual discipleship.

CHAPTER 6

THE CHALLENGE OF AFFLUENCE: REDEFINING WEALTH AND GENEROSITY

As you confront the modern evangelical church's dilemma—its inward focus, escalating operational costs, and the often-minimal allocation of resources to outward-facing mission—you must also directly address one of the most persistent and subtle challenges: the church's relationship with wealth and, specifically, the discipleship of affluent individuals. It is profoundly difficult to build a truly Kingdom-minded church, one characterized by radical generosity and open-handedness, if God has not fundamentally transformed its members' understanding of wealth, shifting their view from earthly accumulation to heavenly treasures.

The tension between earthly possessions and Kingdom priority is not new. Jesus himself confronted this directly in the story of the rich young ruler (Matthew 19:16-26; Mark 10:17-27; Luke 18:18-27). This eager inquirer approached Jesus, seeking the path to eternal life. He boasted of his adherence to the commandments. Yet, Jesus, seeing into his heart, exposed the true idol: "If you wish to be perfect, go, sell your possessions and give to the poor, and you will have treasure in heaven; and come, follow Me". The man walked away saddened, "for he owned much property". This encounter serves as a stark reminder: clinging to temporal wealth can tragically prevent one from truly clinging to Christ and embracing the radical call to discipleship.

This tension is acutely felt by many affluent individuals in the modern church. Often possessing significant business or financial acumen, they look at church budgets dominated by operational costs—new roofs, sound systems, or aesthetic improvements like lobbies—and question the stewardship of potential gifts. They see a system where the vast majority of funds are consumed by internal maintenance rather than external mission. When the church building is not being used as a tool many choose to direct their most significant charitable giving not to the local church's general fund, but to specialized non-profits they perceive as more efficient and impactful—organizations dedicated to fighting human trafficking, [12] providing clean water, or sending underprivileged children to camp. This isn't necessarily a rejection of the church, but a pragmatic decision based on a desire to see their resources generate the greatest possible Kingdom impact. It presents a profound challenge: the church is not only competing for hearts, but also for the trust of its most capable givers.

When the church is at its best example of stewardship of the modern church, particularly in affluent contexts, is to help people redefine their relationship with money, moving away from a culture that relentlessly promotes "more" as the path to happiness. As 1 Timothy 6:17-19 commands, "Instruct those who are rich in this present world not to be conceited or to fix their hope on the uncertainty of riches, but on God, who richly supplies us with all things to enjoy. Instruct them to do good, to be rich in good deeds, to be generous and ready to share, storing up for themselves the treasure of a good foundation for the future, so that they may take hold of that which is truly life".

Organizations like Overflow.co offer Generosity University to work with churches to unlock multiple avenues of generosity. In addition, Generous Giving have done remarkable work in facilitating this transformation, not by asking for money, but by providing a pressure-free environment for individuals to explore the theological underpinnings of generosity. Generous Giving core beliefs emphasize that:

- **Giving is a Heart Issue:** As Jesus taught, "For where your treasure is, there your heart will be also" (Matthew 6:21). Our financial decisions reflect our deepest affections.

- **God Owns It All:** A foundational principle is the recognition that all wealth, resources, and possessions ultimately belong to God. We are merely stewards, entrusted with His resources to be managed according to His direction (1 Chronicles 29:11-14).

- **Heaven, Not Earth, Is Our True Home:** Embracing an eternal perspective allows us to understand that while earthly spending is not inherently wrong, true and lasting treasure is stored in heaven. This heavenly wealth, experienced by us and those reached with the Gospel, ensures for eternity. As Matthew 6:19-20 urges, "Do not store up for yourselves treasures on earth... but store up for yourselves treasures in heaven". This shifts the focus from accumulating perishable assets to investing in eternal impact.

- **Giving Brings Joy:** The act of generosity, rooted in God's prior generosity to us, leads to profound joy, aligning our hearts with God's will and expanding our capacity for blessing.

When we refuse to teach and be discipled in this area, our financial decisions can remain worldly and self-serving, leading to the inward gravitation we see in many churches. The paradox is clear: we cannot serve both God and money (Matthew 6:24). For the church to genuinely reclaim its counter-cultural fierceness and fulfill its outward-facing mission, it must become a community where all members, particularly those with significant resources, are profoundly transformed in their understanding of wealth. This transformation moves them beyond merely tithing or giving out of obligation, to a radical, openhanded generosity that reflects God's heart, lays up treasures in heaven, and powerfully fuels the church's divine assignment to reach the world.

CHAPTER 7

THE HIGH COST OF "CHURCH": FINANCIAL REALITIES AND THE TAX EXEMPTION

Modern churches, regardless of their size, allocate substantial portions of their budget to operational costs. Staff salaries and benefits consistently represent the largest single expenditure, typically averaging between 44% and 49% of the total budget. Building and facility costs—including mortgage or rent, utilities, maintenance, and insurance—constitute another major segment, often around 22% to 25%. Combined, these internal operational categories demonstrably consume the majority of financial resources in most congregations.

The same study indicated a combined 9% was directed towards domestic and international mission support. Research from empty tomb, inc., analyzing 2019 congregational income, found that 84% was spent on internal church activities, leaving approximately 16% for 'the larger mission of the church,' which encompasses various external efforts. [6] Within this, giving to global missions through denominational channels accounted for as little as 2 cents of every dollar received by congregations in 2020. While some churches aspire to dedicate 10% or more of their income to 'missions and charity', and other studies show up to 11-14% of budgets allocated to mission activity outside the congregation or for "mission and benevolence" by evangelical Protestants, these figures often include a broad range of activities, and direct aid to the poor remains strikingly low in many instances. This discrepancy between internal operational spending and external ministry focus highlights a significant area of concern. The discrepancy in some budgets lies in allocating activities like Sunday services, youth group, and children's ministry into the missions budget. While some of these meetings may have an evangelistic message or invitation, they are not considered mission activity.

Recent research reveals a concerning decline in financial giving among evangelical Protestants. The proportion of evangelical adults making a financial donation to a local church fell from 74% to 61% in the past three years (2021-present), and giving to outside charities dropped from 58% to 50%. Average generosity, measured as a proportion of household income given away, decreased from 4% to 3.3% for church and charity combined. Furthermore, the proportion of evangelicals who "tithe" (defined as giving 10% or more of household income) fell from 13% to 10%. This decline is strongly linked to waning spiritual engagement.

The predominant allocation of modern church budgets to internal maintenance—primarily staff salaries and building costs, which together can consume 70-75% or more of expenditures—reflects a deeply institutionalized model. This model, while providing structure and stability, often prioritizes self-perpetuation and internal programming over the radical, outward-focused generosity that characterized the early church. A physical building and its resources can be an incredible asset for ministry—a central hub for the community to worship, fellowship, and engage in outreach. Resources like a kitchen to feed the hungry or a large hall for community gatherings are powerful tools for the church's mission. The building should always remain a tool for the mission. When the mission becomes the building, we have lost our ability to lead with conviction. The financial demands of monthly costs can sometimes become so great that they hinder a church's ability to carry out the mission it so eagerly desires. When we become overcommitted, the focus can dangerously shift from our calling to growing tithes and membership alone. This can lead to a pastor's sermons revolving around fundraising campaigns, tithe, and providing new, "attractional" elements—upgrading the appeal and experience for members. This overwhelming feeling of "keeping up with the Joneses" so people don't leave—the pressure to become funnier, cleverer, or more dynamic to attract more people and retain the ones you have—can lead to mission drift, burnout, and resignations. The varying definitions and reporting of 'charity,' 'benevolence,' and 'missions' can also obscure the true extent of outward giving, potentially masking a systemic issue where a relatively small fraction of funds directly reaches the poor or supports external, frontline missions. The financial data strongly supports the concern that the modern church is 'expensive to run' and often dedicates a disproportionately small percentage of its resources directly to the poor or external missions. With internal operational costs consistently high, the funds allocated for direct benevolence can be as low as 1%, and even broader 'missions' spending, while ranging from approximately 2% for specific categories like global missions via denominations up to a combined 9-14% for wider mission activities in some studies, remains significantly less than internal costs. This financial structure starkly contrasts with the early church's model, where resources were more directly pooled for immediate communal needs and the care of the poor, within a context of simpler living and gathering. The modern church's budget often reflects a model primarily geared towards maintaining an organization and providing services to its members, rather than prioritizing radical external impact. Greater financial transparency and a critical re-evaluation of what constitutes truly outward-focused 'charitable giving' and 'missions' in church budgets are essential for genuine self-assessment and potential reform.

The Question of Pastoral Compensation and Non-Profit Stewardship

While the majority of pastors, particularly those leading small to medium-sized congregations, receive modest salaries reflective of their dedicated service, the issue of pastoral compensation warrants careful consideration within the broader discussion of church finances and non-profit stewardship. Concerns periodically arise, often highlighted by ministry watchdog groups and investigative reports, regarding instances where pastoral compensation packages—especially in some larger churches or media-centric ministries—appear to reach levels that could be deemed exorbitant. These situations, though not representative of the norm, can involve mid to high six-figure salaries, opulent housing allowances, private jet travel, and other significant benefits that stand in stark contrast to the financial realities of average congregants or even other church staff members.

  While the visibility of excessively compensated 'megachurch' leaders can create scandal and rightly prompt questions of stewardship, the reality for the vast majority of pastors is markedly different. Many serve in bi-vocational capacities, or struggle to make ends meet, or face the daunting challenge of providing for their families on modest salaries. Research by Matt Bloom and his team on 'Flourishing in Ministry' provides crucial insights here, highlighting the very real economic and social pressures impacting clergy well-being. Their work underscores that with each passing decade, fewer young people, despite possessing gifts and passions for ministry, are choosing to enter church leadership. This is often due to the perception that vocational ministry offers fewer avenues for significant world impact, comes with diminished public esteem, and frequently entails financial hardship that can make basic life goals, like putting children through school, exceedingly difficult. Bloom's research compellingly argues that addressing the flourishing of those in ministry—not just their financial stability but their overall well-being, sense of purpose, and capacity to thrive—is critical for the church's future health and its ability to attract and retain gifted leaders. This stands in stark contrast to Julian's forced imitations of charity, underscoring that genuine ministerial impact requires sustainable, dignified support, reflecting a 'supernatural value' that permeates all aspects of the church's care for its people. It is important for church workers to receive the average wage of their city as to be able to relate and live amongst its congregants.

As non-profit, tax-exempt organizations, churches operate under a public trust and have an ethical obligation to be responsible stewards of the resources contributed by their members. The Internal Revenue Service (IRS) stipulates that compensation for leaders of non-profits must be "reasonable," meaning it should be comparable to what similarly qualified individuals earn in similar positions at organizations of comparable size and complexity. Compensation deemed "excessive" can lead to penalties and even jeopardize a church's tax-exempt status due to "excess benefit transactions". Organizations like the Evangelical Council for Financial Accountability (ECFA) also require their member organizations to set leadership compensation in a manner demonstrating integrity and propriety, often recommending review and approval by an independent body using comparable data. Reach Right Studios has created a helpful compensation calculator to help churches set appropriate compensation (reachrightstudios.com). The challenge in addressing this issue comprehensively is often compounded by the fact that churches are not required to file IRS Form 990, the informational return that provides financial transparency, including executive compensation, for most other non-profit organizations. This lack of mandatory public disclosure can make it difficult to assess the full scope of compensation in many cases.

Ultimately, the principle of stewardship suggests that no individual leading a non-profit entity, including a church, should become excessively wealthy solely through their position, particularly when such compensation significantly outpaces that of other staff or when resources for ministry and benevolence are constrained. A commitment to transparency, accountability through independent compensation reviews, and a focus on the church's mission over personal enrichment are vital for maintaining trust and integrity. This aligns with the call for the church to model a counter-cultural approach to wealth and resources, reminiscent of the early Galileans' focus on communal care and kingdom priorities rather than personal accumulation.

Table: Modern Evangelical Church Budget Allocation (Average Percentages) (This table aims to synthesize various data points for a general overview. Specific studies may offer more granular breakdowns.)

Category	Average Percentage/ Range	Specific Source Examples/ Notes
Staff Salaries & Benefits	44-49% (can reach ~54% in some analyses)	Christianity Today (2014): 47%; FACTs on Finance (2020 by Lake Institute): 44%; ChurchSalary/Carey Nieuwhof data suggests ~49%.
Building/ Facilities (Mortgage, Utilities, Maintenance, Insurance)	~22-25%	Christianity Today (2014): Sum of categories approx 22% (7% mortgage, 7% utilities, 5% maintenance, 3% insurance); Lake Institute (2020 data) suggests ~25% for facilities.
Internal Programs (Worship, Youth/ Adult Ministry, Admin, Denom. Fees)	~10-15% (variable)	Christianity Today (2014): Sum of relevant categories approx. 12% (Children/Youth 4%, Adult Min 2%, Music/ Worship 2%, Office/Admin 4%, Denom. Fees 3%).
External Missions & Benevolence		
- Direct Benevolence (local aid to the poor/needy)	Often 1% (or a very small unspecified percentage)	Christianity Today (2014): 1%; Tithe.ly notes "a small percentage" for benevolence funds.

- Missions (Domestic & International, various forms)	~2-11% (can be part of a broader ~16% "larger mission" figure)	empty tomb, inc. [6] (2020): 2% for global missions via denominations; Christianity Today (2014): 9% (4% domestic, 5% int'l); Lake Institute (2019 study): 11% for mission activity outside the congregation.
- Total External "Larger Mission" (including the above)	~16%	empty tomb, inc. [6] (2019 data) indicates 16% of congregational income spent on "the larger mission of the church".
Savings/ Reserves	~2% (or recommended 10%)	Christianity Today (2014): 2% for cash reserves; Tithe.ly recommends 10% for savings.
Total Internal Operational Focus (Staff, Building, Internal Prog.)	**~75-84%**	**Implied by subtracting "Larger Mission" (16%) from 100% = 84% (empty tomb, inc. [6]); Lake Institute (2020 data): 50% staff + 25% facilities = 75%.**

The Church's Tax-Exempt Status and the Call for Transparency

The tax-exempt status of churches in the United States has deep historical roots, tracing back to the Roman Emperor Constantine I, who granted the Christian church a complete exemption from all forms of taxation around 312 CE following his supposed conversion. In the U.S., churches were unofficially federally tax-exempt from the nation's founding, with official federal income tax exemption granted in 1894 and reinstated by the Revenue Act of 1913 after an earlier act was declared unconstitutional. The rationale for this exemption is that churches are considered similar to other charities, providing various social services such as shelters, food pantries, and assistance for low-income families, including free after-school programs. Additionally, it is viewed as a means of maintaining the separation of church and state, with churches expected to refrain from political activities in exchange for this status, as per the Johnson Amendment (1954).

Unlike most other non-profits, churches are automatically considered tax-exempt if they meet IRC Section 501(c)(3) requirements and are not required to file IRS Form 990 or 990-EZ, which details their income and financial structure. However, this lack of mandatory financial disclosure has fueled a debate, with some arguing that it grants churches special treatment and can obscure financial abuse. Critics contend that tax exemptions are a form of government subsidy, violating the separation of church and state.

There is a growing call for radical transparency, accountability, and openness in church finances. This includes demands for churches to adopt practices such as regular financial reporting to the congregation, holding open meetings to discuss financial matters, publishing financial statements (e.g., in newsletters or on websites), conducting independent audits, and establishing financial oversight committees. The goal is to ensure that funds are managed responsibly, that the community understands how their contributions are used, and that money can "get in and get out quickly" to serve its intended purpose of mission and benevolence.

PART 3

RECLAIMING THE GALILEAN SPIRIT – A PATH FORWARD FOR A WORLD-TRANSFORMING MOVEMENT

CHAPTER 8

FINANCIAL REFORMATION: PRIORITIZING THE POOR, MISSION, AND RADICAL TRANSPARENCY

Before the church can effectively call its people to a life of radical generosity, it must first look inward and address a painful reality: a widespread and growing crisis of trust. We cannot discuss financial reformation without first acknowledging the reasons people, both inside and outside the church, are hesitant to give. This is not intended as an indictment, but as a necessary and honest admission. For decades, high-profile scandals have rocked the church, creating deep wells of cynicism and suspicion. Stories of financial embezzlement, moral failures and affairs among leaders, doctrinal corruption, and the horrific mishandling of abuse have been widely publicized.

While the vast majority of pastors and churches serve faithfully and with integrity, the actions of a few have tragically jaded the perception of the whole. When people see leaders living in opulent luxury, or hear of funds being used to cover up sin rather than to care for victims, it erodes the moral authority of the entire institution. This makes it incredibly difficult for a faithful pastor to ask for funds for a new roof when a congregant's mind immediately goes to a televangelist's private jet. We must admit that we have problems. The path to reclaiming the trust required for a financial reformation begins with humility, a commitment to unimpeachable integrity, and, most importantly, radical transparency.

A significant path forward for the modern church involves a fundamental financial reformation, shifting priorities to genuinely center the poor and external mission. This requires churches to move beyond merely meeting operational expenses to intentionally and substantially increasing their direct financial contributions to the poor and external missions. This involves a comprehensive re-evaluation of current budget priorities, perhaps aiming for a minimum "tithe" of the church's overall income (e.g., 10-15% or more) specifically for external impact, rather than internal programs that may be broadly categorized as "missions". Practical steps include establishing clear, transparent benevolence policies and robust financial reporting systems that clearly delineate direct aid to the poor from other programmatic expenses. This radical transparency and accountability in financial management, ensuring funds are received and disbursed quickly for their intended purpose, is crucial for building trust and maximizing impact.

Rethinking church budgets also involves challenging the prevailing institutional model where the vast majority of resources are consumed by staff salaries and building maintenance. This necessitates creative solutions for facility use, such as developing multi-purpose spaces, sharing facilities with other organizations, or even considering a return to simpler gathering models where appropriate. Innovative staffing structures that free up funds for outward-facing ministries should also be explored. The overarching goal is to shift the financial center of gravity from internal perpetuation to external transformation.

Furthermore, fostering a theological and spiritual reawakening around radical generosity is crucial. This means moving beyond viewing charity as a discrete "program" or an optional activity, to understanding it as an inherent, non-negotiable expression of Christian faith, mirroring the early church's "supernatural value" of giving. Emphasis should be placed on Jesus's "option for the poor" and the theological imperative of sacrificial giving as central to discipleship. True financial reformation in the modern church necessitates a shift from a purely utilitarian view of money (e.g., "how much do we need to operate?") to a theological one that asks: "How does our collective financial stewardship reflect Christ's identification with the poor and our mandate to be a light to the world?". This requires deep spiritual formation around giving, not just financial planning or budget re-allocation.

The problem, as detailed earlier, is that modern church budgets are demonstrably skewed towards internal costs, with direct financial support for the poor and external missions often constituting a surprisingly small fraction of overall expenditures. Studies reveal that internal operational spending, primarily on staff and facilities, can consume 75% to 84% of a church's income. In stark contrast, direct benevolence to the poor might average as low as 1% of the budget in some analyses, with broader spending on 'the larger mission of the church' (encompassing various external efforts) hovering around 16%. This financial reality stands in sharp contrast to the early church's model of radical generosity, where resources were more directly applied to communal needs and the care of the marginalized, driven by deeply held theological convictions. Therefore, simply reallocating funds, while a necessary step, may not be sufficient. The documented decline in financial giving among some segments of evangelicals has been linked to waning spiritual engagement. To genuinely increase impactful giving to the poor and to mission, the church must re-instill the spiritual motivation and theological imperative for radical generosity that defined the 'impious Galileans'. This implies that financial stewardship is not just about balancing books, but about actively participating in God's redemptive mission in the world. Transparency in financial reporting can build trust and encourage greater, more intentional giving, as members clearly see how their contributions directly align with the church's outward mission.

CHAPTER 9

REVITALIZING EVANGELISM AND COMMUNITY ENGAGEMENT: BECOMING A HUB OF SERVICE

To address the perceived internal focus, the modern church must revitalize its commitment to evangelism and community engagement. This involves empowering lay members for everyday witness, shifting the primary responsibility for evangelism from a select few (clergy, outreach staff) to every believer. Churches should encourage and equip lay members to "gossip the Gospel" in their daily spheres of influence—workplaces, neighborhoods, and social circles—through personal witness and reasoned defense (apologetics). This includes providing practical training on how to integrate faith conversations into everyday life.

While emphasizing individual witness, churches should also develop strategic, community-focused outreach programs that genuinely address felt needs within their local contexts. These programs should move beyond mere attendance-driven events to tangible acts of service and compassion, mirroring the early church's organized care for widows, strangers, and the marginalized. This includes fostering partnerships with local organizations and actively seeking opportunities to serve the broader community.

A crucial step is shifting metrics from solely attendance to transformative impact. Churches should re-evaluate what constitutes "success". Instead of primarily focusing on internal metrics like Sunday attendance numbers and small group participation rates, they should prioritize metrics that reflect outward impact: new conversions, demonstrable community transformation, tangible aid provided to the poor, and the overall missional engagement of members. This shift in focus will naturally realign resources and energy towards external outcomes.

From "Come" to "Go": The Church as the People of God in the Community

For many decades, a dominant model in numerous church contexts has been the "come congregation" or attractional approach. This model, often unintentionally, centers its primary energy and resources on drawing people to the church's physical location and into its internal programs. Success is frequently measured by the number of attendees, the size of the membership roll, and the vibrancy of activities within the church walls. While fellowship and corporate worship are vital, an overemphasis on this "come and see what we offer" approach can inadvertently create a divide between "church life" and "real life," potentially limiting the church's broader transformative impact on the surrounding community.

A vital shift in perspective, articulated by leaders like Pastor Roger Valci, calls for embracing the identity of a "go congregation". This is not merely a semantic change; it represents a fundamental reorientation of the church's mission and understanding of itself. In the "go congregation" model, the church is not primarily a destination people arrive at, but a dynamic body of believers who are equipped, empowered, and sent out to be the living presence of Christ within their neighborhoods, workplaces, schools, and social spheres. The pastor's role, in this framework, leans heavily into the Ephesians 4 model: equipping the saints for the work of ministry, rather than being the primary service provider to a passive audience. The focus moves from gathering people into a sacred space to mobilizing people from a sacred space into a needy world.

This "go" mentality finds strong resonance with the growth and expansion of the early church. The initial explosion of the Christian faith was not built on attracting large crowds to magnificent edifices. Instead, it was a decentralized, relational movement where the life and witness of believers permeated their *oikoi*—their households, extended families, and spheres of influence. Their radical love, sacrificial service, and tangible care for the vulnerable within the community (actions that even an adversary like Julian the Apostate had to acknowledge) made them a compelling and credible force. People were drawn to the faith and into fellowship often because they first encountered Christ through Christians in their daily lives. The growth was organic, often moving from the outside-in, as transformed lives in the community led to the formation of new house-based assemblies.

Embracing the identity of a "go congregation" has profound implications:

- **Ministry Redefined:** Ministry ceases to be an activity confined to church-sanctioned programs or performed only by "professionals." It becomes the everyday actions, conversations, and vocational callings of every believer, wherever God has placed them.

- **Leadership Refocused:** Church leaders see their primary task as discipleship that equips and empowers the congregation for their mission in the world, discerning where God is at work in the community and mobilizing believers to join Him there.

- **Structures Reimagined:** Church structures become more flexible, decentralized, and geared towards supporting and resourcing initiatives that emerge from the congregation's engagement with community needs, rather than solely maintaining internal programs.

- **Metrics Realigned:** While gathering for worship and fellowship remains important, success is increasingly measured by external impact: lives transformed within the community, tangible needs being met, believers actively and confidently living out their faith in their influence, and the overall spiritual and social health of the neighborhood or city improving.

This outward, "go" orientation is also foundational for effective "city movements"—collaborative efforts where multiple churches and Christian organizations work together for the holistic transformation of their urban environment. Such movements, sometimes discussed in contexts like Transforming the Bay with Christ (tbc.city), Palau City Movements (Palau.org), For Charolotte (forcharlotte.org) or similiar city focused coalitions, recognize that the complex challenges of a city require a unified, multi-faceted response from the Body of Christ. Using tools like Barna (barna.com) and GLOO (gloo.com) for data are critical to learn for about your city. This necessitates believers being deeply embedded and actively engaged in all societal domains—business, arts, education, government, healthcare, social services—living out their faith redemptively and working for the common good, the *shalom*, of their city. The goal extends beyond individual conversions to fostering environments where all people can flourish.

Ultimately, the "impious Galileans" were a "go congregation" par excellence. They didn't wait for the world to come to them; they went into the world, and their distinct, Christ-centered way of life, their radical compassion, and their unwavering witness had a profound, society-shaping impact. For the modern church to reclaim this kind of counter-cultural, transformative presence, it must be willing to move beyond a purely attractional mindset. It must embrace the call to "go," empowering every member to be the church in the community, carrying the fierce and tender love of Christ into every corner of a watching and wounded world.

This shift requires us to ask a hard question about our church culture. Are we operating like a members-only country club or a Trader Joe's (a popular west coast of American grocery chain)? The country club model is exclusive; it exists for the comfort and preference of its existing members. The danger of this model is that it can create an artificial reality, a manicured bubble completely insulated from the grit, pain, and diversity of the world outside its walls. Life inside this bubble becomes an echo chamber, where the focus shifts to maintaining the clubhouse, perfecting the member experience, and ensuring everyone is comfortable. It inadvertently traps people in a world that isn't real, fostering a faith that is unprepared for hardship and unburdened by the call to the marginalized. Outreach can become less about a desperate rescue mission and more like offering an occasional day pass, vetting prospective people to see if they'll fit in and can afford the dues. Its primary goal, often unspoken, is to keep existing members happy and secure. By contrast, consider the culture of a Trader Joe's. It's a place bustling with energy. People are there because they all agree on the value of the product. They are genuinely happy to be there, the employees are helpful, and you often see people helping each other in the aisles. It's a friendly, no-frills, mission-focused environment. Crucially, people go to get what they need—good nourishment—and then they leave, equipped to go live their lives. A church with a Trader Joe's culture is not trying to trap people inside; it's a joyful supply station for the mission, equipping people with spiritual truth and authentic community so they can then go out into the world. The "impious Galileans" ran a Trader Joe's, not a country club.

My father, Tom Brock, would often preach a simple but profound truth. He would say that when a new baby, everything changes. Even the grouchiest person in the corner melts; everyone wants to see, hold, and delight in the new life. That baby becomes the joyful center of attention, reminding everyone of the wonder of birth. He taught me that the church desperately needs to be infused with "new babies"—new

THE IMPIOUS GALILEANS

Christ Followers coming into the Kingdom. A church without a steady stream of new Christ Followers risks becoming sterile and joyless. New converts are the lifeblood of a healthy church for several reasons. They ask the foundational questions that force the spiritually mature to remember their "first love." Their raw testimonies and contagious passion for Jesus can melt cynicism and break down established cliques. A new baby in Christ unifies the church family in a common, joyful purpose: to nurture, protect, and disciple this precious new life. A constant influx of "new babies" keeps a church healthy, vibrant, and focused on the basics of the Gospel, preventing it from becoming an institution that exists only for itself.

This book is, in many ways, the product of a personal and ministry-wide journey. After starting as a junior high pastor and working my way through multiple roles—from teaching and preaching to teaching a Bible college course and young adults ministry—I found myself, after nearly eight years, gripped by a profound conviction. I felt a deep, internal call to live out my ministry through my life, not just through my preaching. As I looked out one Sunday evening after preaching I realized that the people were spiritually equipped, knowledgeable of the word, and they did not need more messages, they needed to use all that they had learned. Most church members attend on Sunday, have bible classes on Tuesdays, small groups on Wednesday nights, Thursday is often a womens or mens bible study, Friday outreaches, Saturday prayer meeting or conference time, and repeat. We had created no time for the "go". In fact we consumed the church with programs, special interest groups, events, and most of them lived at the church! I wanted to see more and different for my ministry. I was compelled to serve my city and to truly reach the community around us. This conviction was sharpened by the words of the late urban ministry pioneer Ray Bakke, who shared that when a church moves in an area the property taxes go up and often a neighborhood may loose a grocery store, warehouse, or other buildings

74

that often get converted to a church building taking a way valuable retail space meant to serve the community. The reason the taxes go up because the church is tax exempt and the home owners and business absorb the loss in property taxes. The Governments thinking was that when a church truly moves into a neighborhood, the property values should go up, not because of the building, but because the church provides such overwhelming resources and care to the community that it saves the city money. The least the state could do, in that scenario, is not charge the church taxes. As I further researched it was called "the halo effect", churches were meant to glow with resources and care for their community. This idea was both inspiring and convicting, are we adding value to our neighbors, property value, and meeting needs in our immediate area? I was part of a medium-large church, but like many, most of our congregants commuted from across the city; we weren't truly embedded in the immediate, taxable area we occupied. After discussions with our staff, we made a decisive shift. I became the community pastor, and we resurrected an old 501(c)(3) community-based organization the church had set up years prior. I remember the initial excitement of this new direction. I was so anxious to meet with the mayor of our city—the eighth largest in the U.S.—and tell him that our church had committed full-time to serving our community. My excitement, however, was short-lived. I passionately shared my story and our new vision, the mayor delivered a humbling rebuke. He told me that, in his experience, Christians were "all passion and no power". He had seen groups get excited about causes like breast cancer awareness or anti-human trafficking. They would wear the colored bracelets, hold a big event, and then, just as quickly, forget the cause, making little to no lasting impact. He was right. So much of what we had done in the past was fleeting.

After much conversation and prayer we started with what we had. We had a building that we could commit more to the community and youth, use the children's and youth space we already had but improve it greatly. We dedicated a good amount of our building to be used for our neighbors, for the majority of the week. We started providing child care for infants to 5 years old. It was not rocket science or deeply systemic in nature, but very practical: affordable childcare, and extracurricular activities like music lessons, martial arts, and even a skate park for kids who otherwise had no access. Our neighbors did not have access to many of the extra curricular activities due to budget cuts the surrounding schools amongst, they removed most of the music, sports, and after school programs. It especially met a need for pre eduction years families and for youth that did not have a place to go to after school. Later, we built a park and playground to be even more inviting. We served our community well, earning several awards for our childcare center and, most importantly, began to truly get to know our neighbors. Sadly many of our neighbors did not know we were in their neighborhood until we opened the doors they were looking for and needed. It was maybe a year later, I spoke to the mayor again. As I remember it was like a call from the commissioner that and I had been anxiously awaiting. It was our chance to respond like Batman to a big problem. It went something like this, "I'm aware you've done several anti-human trafficking fundraisers, and I have a human trafficking problem". Our large city, with its multiple ports of entry, a high amount of expendable income, and a police force undergoing pension reform, losing nearly a thousand officers. The city was seeing human trafficking at an all-time high. The Mayor needed expert advice. As a church, we sadly had none. We could certainly preach morality to congregants and deter future "johns", a name given to buyers of exploited persons. We could raise more money for international efforts, increase prayer, or create sermons to spread the news, but it did not seem to be close to what they envisioned and desperately needed. After much thought and prayer we thought of a good fit for the city. For years, we had been supporting James and Athena Pond of the former Transitions Global, who had done incredible work in Cambodia for over a decade, achieving a remarkable 10%, recidivism rate for victims coming out of their program. They were true subject matter experts on their program and programs around the world. Our church put out the call to the congregants and raised the money to bring them in to conduct feasibility study. Over the next three months, James, Athena, and I met with a staggering array of stakeholders: members of Congress, state Senators, the FBI, the District Attorney's Office, the Department of Family and Children's Services, the Police Chief, Juvenile Hall, Judges, and leaders from non-profits and care centers across the City and County. We didn't come with answers; we came to listen and to learn. We did not gather them at our church, "book end" our meetings with prayer, nor did we evangelize anyone in particular. We attempted to join the work that so many amazing Christian and non Christians had been doing for decades. I did not wear my best suit and ask them to address me as pastor, we went where the problem lied and where problem solvers were. After a few months of research and strategy all the information was aggregated into a comprehensive nearly 50 page report, outlining best practices for policy, protocol, adjudication, and aftercare for victims, based on their experience and data from over 300 shelters and anti-trafficking organizations worldwide. We then gifted this to our city leaders and friends in the space that serve so diligently. Following this we then did what we as a church knew how to do. We gathered all those leaders back together—the Senators, Police Chiefs, FBI Special Agents, Social Services Directors and Chief of our Child Protection Agency and all who were interviewed—we served a beautiful meal, gave a gift to every attendee and delivered the results from all of the research they and we had done. We showed radical hospitality in an event that was second to none—thanks to Shiloh Events, a Christian woman in the church that donated her gifts to produce the whole event. We honored our Police Chief for his efforts and we recognized every official and leader in the room. We showed radical generosity and made friends. We didn't ultimately solve human trafficking that day. When asked why we did this, we said God cares about these victims deeply and so do we. We listened. We contributed.

We used our resources to get data that no one had ever had the time or the finances to ascertain. We partnered with first in class, hard working professionals to give the city our best. We embraced the call from Jeremiah to "seek the peace and prosperity of the city... Pray to the Lord for it, because if it prospers, you too will prosper" (Jeremiah 29:7). Our work had accelerated the work in our city for those who were being victimized. We remained involved and helped create robust partnerships, forged resources for a aftercare centers that would be victim centered and ran by professional in the space. We had become a church of our city. We weren't in competition with our city; we didn't seek to be better than, or even to be seen by it. We simply sought to join in its peace and transformation. It was from that moment I knew I wanted to be an "impious Galilean" and see the church become a force that transforms cities.

The objective is not merely to add "more evangelism" programs to the church calendar, but to cultivate a missional culture where outward focus is an inherent part of the church's identity and every member's discipleship. This means that internal spiritual growth must actively propel believers into external engagement. If discipleship within a sermon or small group is not frequently equipping and motivating members for external mission, it can inadvertently contribute to an insular community. Our attendance grew in those years following the work, particularly among the young adult generation. It changed their perceived notion that the church was only interested in itself. They were ignited to serve a real God, with an active faith, and be known for their love in the community. The "impious Galileans" were distinct precisely because they engaged the world with their radical faith, not retreated from it. The transformation requires a conscious effort to integrate mission into every aspect of church life and individual discipleship.

Galileans Ministered in Community to Reach Community: A Call to Radical Outwardness

We have explored the historical distinctives of the early "impious Galileans"—their audacious generosity, their communal solidarity, and their unyielding commitment to a Kingdom that stood in stark contrast to the prevailing Roman order. We have confronted the uncomfortable truths of our modern expressions of faith, often characterized by inward gravitation and the maintenance of institutional structures. Now, let us reflect on the profound imperative that defined those who first followed the Galilean.

The very foundation of our calling comes from Jesus himself: "Come after Me [as disciples—letting Me be your Guide], follow Me, and I will make you fishers of men!" (Matthew 4:19). We are called to evangelism and reaching out to those who do not know Christ. For decades, our vision of evangelism has often been shaped by approaches like street preaching, Jesus Movement crusades (right for its day and time), altar calls, or simply passing out tracts. But if we are indeed called to be fishers of men, why are we not catching fish? Perhaps we are trying to evangelize the wrong way. Maybe we are not called to reach people as a solo effort. The biblical perspective of fishing for souls—the story of the great catch—suggests something far more expansive than a solitary figure with a rod and tackle box, patiently choosing a lure, casting, and reeling. It suggests a commercial shrimp boat with nets spread wide. This is the essence of the "hook verses nets approach", a concept eloquently written by Robert Crosby in Outreach Magazine many years ago. [13]

Shifting Mindsets: From Pole to Net Evangelism

Breaking the fear often associated with evangelism involves adopting a "net mentality". Consider the contrast between pole fishing and net fishing mindsets and how a communitarian effort can help people get "caught into a community":

Pole Fishing	Net Fishing
is a solo effort.	is a team effort.
involves throwing them a line on your own.	involves showing them Christ within a community.
helps people hear about the gospel.	helps people see the gospel lived out.
is about "coming to a decision."	is about "coming into community."
is convincing them of the truth of Christ (information).	is showing to them the love of Christ (transformation).
tends to view evangelism as an event.	tends to view evangelism as a process.
focuses on getting them to say "yes."	focuses on getting them to "come and see."
may result in decisions.	results in disciples.
is about "catching" them.	is about "keeping" them.

This table clarifies why our traditional approaches often fall short. We've been "pole fishing" individually for decisions, when Jesus called us to "net fishing" for disciples in community. This isn't just about catching them; it's about keeping them, bringing them into the transformative embrace of a genuine community.

The Catch: Hated for the Right Reason

And here, my friend, is the profound truth, the uncomfortable catch that confronts us all: The early church was not hated for being irrelevant. It was hated for being profoundly, unsettlingly, and undeniably relevant. It was hated because its fierce love, its radical generosity, and its uncompromising allegiance to Christ exposed the moral bankruptcy of the empire. They were hated for demonstrating a better way of living, a more compelling vision of community, a deeper source of truth that challenged the very foundations of power and privilege.

We have often feared being hated, and in that fear, we have too frequently chosen comfort and cultural accommodation. We have longed for acceptance, and in doing so, we have inadvertently surrendered the very distinctiveness that made us a transforming force. The true "catch" for us today is this: Until we are willing to be hated for our radical love, our audacious generosity, our unwavering commitment to justice, and our fearless proclamation of Christ's Kingdom—until we are willing to be hated for the right reasons—we will never truly reclaim the counter-cultural fierceness of those "impious Galileans". We will never truly minister in community to genuinely reach the community around us.

Reclaiming the Outward Imperative: A Call to Go and Do

This is our collective call to action—a profound mission that is our very identity as a community: to reach people with the love of Christ. This mission requires a patient, inconvenient love, one that moves beyond a social club and into authentic, life-on-life relationships. We are called to build bridges, not walls. By inviting the unreached into our lives, we demonstrate a love that breaks down barriers. Be mindful of the enemy's tactics; don't allow offenses, politics, or socio-economic class to become snares that hinder your outreach. Instead, exercise wisdom and boldness. Our personal and collective testimony is a powerful gateway to freedom, so be prepared to share it.

The early followers of Jesus, the "Impious Galileans," didn't compartmentalize their lives. There was no "ministry time" and "secular time." Their faith permeated every aspect of their existence—from their work to their family life. This integrated approach meant their witness was authentic and powerful. Their lives were the sermon. This is a stark contrast to a poor witness, which often stems from a disconnect between what is professed on Sunday and what is practiced on Monday. When we bifurcate our lives, we create a gap that can easily be filled with hypocrisy. This not only discredits the individual but, more importantly, can deter others from considering the message of Christ. A powerful witness, like that of the Galileans, is one where a person's life and testimony are in complete alignment. Their actions and words are consistent, demonstrating a faith that is not just a set of beliefs but a living, breathing reality.

The Galilean model was always a communal one—community ministering to community, families reaching families. You are not an individual sent out alone, but an integral part of a collective mission. This unified front provides strength, accountability, and a powerful picture of what life in Christ looks like. When a community reaches out to another community, it's a living testament to the power of shared faith. To be effective in this mission, we must be rooted in this kind of integrated, communal faith. Consume the Word, walk in the Spirit, and remain in fellowship with other believers. This prepares you to share the message of Jesus with clarity and conviction. Don't let a poor witness disqualify you from being a vessel for God. This is a call to the church community to go and do. Be bold in your confession, committed to your mission, and relentless in your pursuit of results. It's time to pick up your part of the net, to proclaim and pray. This is our transformative power, the very way the Galileans ministered in community to reach their community.

What does this "net" look like in practice?

- **Become a Living Testimony:** The church community should function as a beacon of Jesus' love. It's a place where the unchurched can feel comfortable, belong, learn about Christ, and ultimately be transformed. Our communal life itself is a powerful witness.

- **Build Authentic Relationships:** Intentionally invite the unreached into your life and the life of your community. Avoid creating walls or offenses that can be used by the enemy to hinder outreach. This requires wisdom and an open heart.

- **Share Your Personal Story:** Your testimony is a powerful gateway to someone else's freedom. Be bold and ready to share how Jesus has worked in your life, as this personal narrative can be incredibly compelling.

- **Be Prepared and Consistent:** To share the message of Jesus effectively, you must be prepared. This means walking in the Spirit, consistently consuming the Word, and maintaining fellowship with other believers. A consistent, integrated witness—where your life aligns with your beliefs—is essential.

- **Embrace the Mission:** This is a call to go and do. Be bold in your confession of faith, committed to the mission of outreach, and unwavering in your pursuit of results. It is time to pick up your part of the net.

When we embrace this collective mission, as per Mark 16:15-17: "He said to them, 'Go into all the world and preach the gospel to all creation. Whoever believes and is baptized will be saved, but whoever does not believe will be condemned. And these signs will accompany those who believe: In my name they will drive out demons; they will speak in new tongues...'". This endeavor will require profound love— patient, enduring, and a willingness to be inconvenienced. As a church, we ask God, What is our calling as a community? Each member must pick up their part of the net.

As an impious Galilean, our lives become marked by a counter-culturalism and kindness that radiates the love of God.

CHAPTER 10

CULTIVATING ANCIENT DISCIPLINES FOR MODERN DISCIPLESHIP: CHARACTER, BELIEF SYSTEMS, AND COUNTER-CULTURAL KINDNESS

A return to the foundational character and disciplines of the early "impious Galileans" is essential for the modern church's revitalization. This includes embracing simplicity and contentment, encouraging a return to this early Christian value, directly challenging the pervasive consumerism and materialism often found within modern society and, by extension, the church. This involves intentional teaching on contentment, the dangers of wealth, and the willingness to live with less, even to the point of giving away possessions for the sake of the Kingdom (Acts 4:32-35). The church must equip its people to be godly, not nationalist, not conformist, but truly counter-cultural in their kindness.

Strengthening communal accountability and mutual care is also vital. This means re-emphasizing the profound importance of genuine communal accountability and mutual care within the body of believers. It involves actively implementing principles of moral discipline, drawing from the tiered approach outlined in Matthew 18:15-17, with a consistent focus on restoration and reconciliation. Fostering authentic "siblingship" that extends practical, emotional, and spiritual support will mirror the strong internal cohesion and mutual aid observed in the early church.

Deepening spiritual practices such as prayer, scripture engagement, and fasting is paramount. This involves prioritizing the foundational spiritual disciplines that shaped the early church. These include consistent, fervent prayer (e.g., praying the Lord's Prayer multiple times daily, constant prayer), deep engagement with Scripture (including memorization and meditation), and regular, intentional fasting. These practices should be taught and practiced not as legalistic duties, but as vital means of spiritual formation, empowerment for mission, and cultivation of a distinct, Christ-like character.

These ancient practices find a modern echo in the work of leaders like Randy Frazee. [14] Through tools like the Congregational Life Profile, Frazee's work emphasizes the need for a balanced, holistic discipleship. This framework assesses the health of believers across key relationships: their relationship with God (Up), their connection with fellow believers (In), and their mission to the world (Out). The "impious Galileans" were a living embodiment of this balance. Their deep spiritual practices nurtured their life with God (Up), their robust communal accountability forged their life together (In), and their zealous evangelism and radical charity defined their life in the world (Out). They were not strong in one area to the detriment of the others; their faith was an integrated whole.

The early church's rigorous internal discipline and consistent spiritual practices were not merely personal piety but a collective commitment that made them distinct, credible, and compelling to outsiders, including Julian. This internal strength and coherence were the wellspring from which their radical generosity and zealous evangelism flowed. If the modern church perceives itself as having "lost its way" in external impact, the underlying cause may reside in a weakening of these foundational internal disciplines and communal accountability. Reclaiming the "impious Galilean" identity therefore necessitates a renewed commitment to these often-unseen, fundamental practices that shape individual and communal character, recognizing that internal vitality is a prerequisite for sustained external influence.

Further reflections on this highlight the importance of cultivating an "others-first unity" and a "Kingdom first" mindset, which directly aligns with the idea of counter-cultural kindness and disciplined community. There is an emphasis that "allegiance to Christ supersedes our many differences" and that true collaboration means little concern "about which organization got the credit for lives changed". This spirit of selflessness and shared purpose is crucial for the internal health and external impact of the church.

CHAPTER 11

RESTORING THE FOUNDATIONS: THE VITAL AND SUPPORTED ROLES OF APOSTLES, PROPHETS, AND EVANGELISTS TODAY

Introduction: The Missing Architects and Messengers

The contemporary evangelical church, as we've explored, stands at a crossroads, often grappling with a sense of deviation from its foundational principles and a dilution of its counter-cultural impact. We've drawn inspiration from the early "impious Galileans," whose fierce faith and radical practices challenged their world. A critical component of that early dynamism was the active presence and function of all the ministry gifts bestowed upon the church. The Apostle Paul, in his letter to the Ephesians, outlines these divine endowments: "And He Himself gave some to be apostles, some prophets, some evangelists, and some pastors and teachers, for the equipping of the saints for the work of ministry, for the edifying of the body of Christ" (Ephesians 4:11-12 NKJV). These gifts were not meant to be hierarchical titles but functional roles, essential for the church's health, growth, and capacity to fulfill its mission.

However, a candid assessment of many modern church structures reveals an operational emphasis that, while valuing the crucial roles of pastors and teachers, often inadvertently sidelines or misunderstands the equally vital functions of apostles, prophets, and evangelists. Just as the early church's reputation was forged by the radical character and actions of its people, so too is the modern church's potential impact intrinsically linked to the full expression of these God-given ministries. This chapter will delve into the critical, yet often neglected, roles of the apostle, prophet, and evangelist. We will explore how their marginalization has impacted the church's mission and argue for the necessity of their active, recognized, and financially supported presence. For if the church is to reclaim the "fierce movement" quality of the original "impious Galileans", it must be willing to restore and empower all the foundational gifts designed to build and mobilize it.

The Modern Dilemma: Marginalization and Misunderstanding

The vibrant, multifaceted leadership structure envisioned in the New Testament, designed to equip believers and extend the Kingdom, has in many instances become narrowed. This has led to a situation where key governmental and missional gifts—specifically those of the apostle, prophet, and evangelist—are often misunderstood, underutilized, or pushed to the fringes of the institutional church.

- **The Disenfranchised Evangelist:** The modern evangelist often finds themselves operating as a "parachurch ministry," feeling cut off from the local church body. This term "disenfranchise" aptly describes a cutting off from the legal privilege and right to be an integral part of the church's core operations. Often, churches position evangelists "outside" because their impact cannot be easily quantified within typical metrics for church growth or fit neatly into strategic planning for Sunday services. This separation carries significant negative consequences. Firstly, new believers who come to faith through the efforts of these often-itinerant evangelists may not be effectively connected to local churches for the crucial process of discipleship, potentially creating "spiritual orphans". The evangelist, gifted in proclamation, is not typically equipped or positioned to be the long-term discipler or pastor. Secondly, this model forces those called to be "full-time soul savers" into the exhausting role of "full-time fundraisers". They are compelled to continually seek support from various churches, a method that is often uncomfortable, unsustainable, and falls short of providing consistent, dignified remuneration. This financial precariousness can lead to a stagnation of evangelistic outreach, as the church system itself isn't structured to sustain and propel this gift. The lack of consistent support can stifle the very gift the church desperately needs, preventing gifted individuals from committing to full-time evangelism if they lack financial security for their families.

- **The Silenced Prophet:** The prophetic gift, intended to bring divine guidance, edification, exhortation, comfort (1 Corinthians 14:3), and at times, necessary course correction to the church, also faces significant challenges in the contemporary setting. A fear of the mystical, concerns about potential misuse or emotionalism, or simply a lack of understanding of its proper function can lead to the prophet being silenced or relegated to the margins. While discernment is undeniably crucial in stewarding any spiritual gift, an overemphasis on control or a discomfort with direct divine address can create an environment where prophetic voices are not cultivated, recognized, or heeded. The early church, however, operated with the understanding that prophecy, when rightly expressed and judged, was vital for its spiritual health and direction. If the modern church seeks to navigate complex cultural waters and discern God's specific will for its communities, it must learn to create safe, accountable spaces for genuine prophetic ministry to flourish, rather than defaulting to a skepticism that quenches the Spirit.

- **The Grounded Apostle:** The term "apostle" is often associated exclusively with the original twelve disciples of Jesus or Paul. While their role was unique and foundational in an absolute sense (Ephesians 2:20), the apostolic *function* or *gifting* continues to be essential for the church. This gift manifests in areas such as pioneering new missional works, laying spiritual foundations in new believers or churches, providing spiritual parenting and oversight to leaders and ministries, ensuring doctrinal integrity, and offering strategic, "master-builder" (1 Corinthians 3:10) wisdom for the broader body of Christ. In many contemporary church contexts, these apostolic functions may be diffuse, informally attempted by other primary giftings, or altogether absent. This can result in churches that lack a pioneering spirit, struggle with doctrinal drift, or fail to reproduce and expand their kingdom impact effectively. Without the intentional recognition and empowerment of apostolic leadership, the church may find itself maintaining the status quo rather than boldly advancing into new territories, much like the "impious Galileans" did in their own challenging context.

The marginalization of these three crucial gifts—evangelist, prophet, and apostle—results in a church that is not fully equipped to fulfill its mandate. It contributes to the "internal gravitation" and "missional drift" discussed earlier in this book, hindering the church from becoming the dynamic, world-transforming movement it is called to be.

Biblical Mandate for Support: "The Laborer is Worthy of His Wages"

It is not enough to simply acknowledge the importance of the apostolic, prophetic, and evangelistic gifts; the church must also grapple with its responsibility to materially support those who are called to function in these capacities. The Scriptures are clear that those who dedicate their lives to the ministry of the Gospel have a right to receive their living from the Gospel. The Apostle Paul, when defending his own apostleship and right to support, asked rhetorically, "Who ever goes to war at his own expense? Who plants a vineyard and does not eat of its fruit? Or who tends a flock and does not drink of the milk of the flock?" (1 Corinthians 9:7 NKJV). He further argues from the Law of Moses and ultimately from the Lord's own ordinance: "Even so the Lord has commanded that those who preach the gospel should live from the gospel" (1 Corinthians 9:14 NKJV).

This principle is not limited to those who serve as pastors or teachers within a local congregation. It extends to all who labor faithfully in proclaiming and building up the church. Consider the words to Timothy, "Let the elders who rule well be counted worthy of double honor, especially those who labor in the word and doctrine. For the Scripture says, 'You shall not muzzle an ox while it treads out the grain,' and, 'The laborer is worthy of his wages'" (1 Timothy 5:17-18 NKJV). The "labor" described here encompasses the diverse work of building up the body of Christ, a work in which apostles, prophets, and evangelists are key participants. Jesus Himself affirmed this when sending out His disciples, stating, "for the laborer is worthy of his wages" (Luke 10:7 NKJV).

Yet, a common and detrimental disparity exists in many church circles: while pastors often receive salaries (however modest they may sometimes be), evangelists, and frequently prophets and those functioning apostolically, are often expected to operate on "charity" or intermittent love offerings. This model can force individuals, who should be dedicated to their unique callings, into a near-constant state of fundraising. Imagine an evangelist, burning with a passion to reach the lost, yet spending the majority of their time and energy trying to secure enough funds to provide for their family. This is not merely an inconvenience; it is an injustice that stifles the effective operation of these essential gifts. Financial insecurity can prevent gifted individuals from fully stepping into their callings, or it can distract and diminish the impact of those who do. If the church is to see these foundational ministries restored to their rightful place and effectiveness, it must move beyond a paradigm that essentially outsources their financial well-being. Acknowledging that "the laborer is worthy of his wages" requires a practical commitment to structuring financial support for those whom God has given as apostles, prophets, and evangelists, enabling them to minister freely and powerfully, without the crushing burden of financial instability. This is not about creating lucrative positions, but about providing dignified, consistent support so that these ministers can devote themselves wholeheartedly to the "work of ministry" for which they have been called and gifted.

Reintegrating and Empowering: A Path Forward

Recognizing the problem of marginalized foundational gifts and understanding the biblical mandate for their support is only the first step. The church must then actively work to reintegrate and empower apostles, prophets, and evangelists, creating an environment where these ministries can thrive and contribute fully to the "equipping of the saints for the work of ministry". This involves intentional shifts in culture, structure, and resource allocation.

- **For Evangelists:** The call for the church is to bring the evangelist back from the periphery and into the heart of its mission and operational strategy. This means more than occasional invitations to speak; it means considering evangelists as integral staff members, providing them with consistent salaries and the resources necessary to focus on their primary calling: reaching the unreached. Imagine the potential for revival if churches were to truly champion and release their evangelists, creating a supportive environment where a flood of unbelievers could be brought into loving communities to hear the Gospel. Churches should value the evangelist's primary role in outreach, not as an auxiliary function, but as a core component of a healthy, growing body that is serious about the Great Commission. This allows the evangelist to move from being a "full-time fundraiser" to a full-time "fisher of men", partnering with the local body to both "catch" and "keep" new believers within a discipling community.

- **For Prophets:** Reintegrating the prophetic gift requires cultivating a culture of honor and discernment. This means teaching congregations about the nature and purpose of New Testament prophecy—which is primarily for edification, exhortation, and comfort (1 Corinthians 14:3)—while also establishing clear, biblical protocols for how prophetic words are shared, weighed, and responded to. Churches can actively identify, nurture, and provide appropriate platforms for individuals with recognized prophetic gifts. This doesn't necessarily mean a formal "office" in every case, but it does mean creating space in gatherings, leadership meetings, and strategic planning processes for prophetic insight to be shared and considered. When stewarded wisely, the prophetic gift can bring vital clarity, warning, encouragement, and course correction, helping the church align more closely with God's specific intentions and avoid the pitfalls of mere human strategizing or cultural conformity.

- **For Apostles:** Empowering apostolic ministry often begins with recognizing that this function extends beyond church planting, though that is a key aspect. It involves identifying and commissioning individuals who carry an apostolic grace for foundational building, spiritual parenting and oversight to leaders and ministries, ensuring doctrinal integrity, and offering strategic, "master-builder" (1 Corinthians 3:10) wisdom for the broader body of Christ. In many contemporary church contexts, these apostolic functions may be diffuse, informally attempted by other primary giftings, or altogether absent. This can result in churches that lack a pioneering spirit, struggle with doctrinal drift, or fail to reproduce and expand their kingdom impact effectively. Without the intentional recognition and empowerment of apostolic leadership, the church may find itself maintaining the status quo rather than boldly advancing into new territories, much like the "impious Galileans" did in their own challenging context.

By intentionally creating structures and cultures that recognize, support, and release these foundational gifts, the church moves closer to functioning as the fully equipped, dynamic body Christ intends it to be. This is not about elevating certain individuals, but about stewarding all of God's gifts for the common good and the advancement of His Kingdom.

Conclusion: Towards a Fully Equipped and Fierce Church

The journey of the modern church back to a state of "impious Galilean" fierceness—a radical, counter-cultural witness that transforms communities and challenges the status quo—is multifaceted. It involves a deep re-examination of our internal character, our communal practices, our financial stewardship, and, as we have explored in this chapter, our very leadership structures. The restoration of apostles, prophets, and evangelists to their rightful, recognized, and supported places within the church is not a minor theological adjustment; it is a strategic imperative for unlocking the full potential and power God intends for His body.

When we fail to embrace this divinely architected team model, we inadvertently foster the phenomenon of personality-driven churches—often becoming "one-man shows" where the health, growth, and spiritual depth of the congregation are limited by the strengths and weaknesses of a single individual. Such a church is chronically disadvantaged, operating with perhaps only one-fifth of the leadership gifting God intends for its full development and mission. If a church is predominantly led by a pastor, it may excel in nurturing and care but lack outward evangelistic thrust or pioneering apostolic vision. If guided primarily by a teacher, it might become strong in doctrine and structure but miss the prophet's timely warnings and edification, or the evangelist's passion for the lost. A prophet at the helm might bring powerful words of edification or course correction but struggle to implement practical training or consistent discipleship. An evangelist-led community, while fervent in outreach, may lack deep discipleship structures and a focus beyond its immediate context. Similarly, an apostle-led church might focus so intently on the broader kingdom plan for the region that the internal care and specific needs of the local flock are underdeveloped. We simply miss the holistic expression of Christ's body and the comprehensive equipping of the saints when key leadership positions are vacant or their functions ignored.

Why, then, would any church choose a model that resembles a monarchy, where singular leadership overshadows the diverse, complementary gifts God has ordained for His people's flourishing and His mission's success? When these foundational gifts are active, honored, and resourced, the church ceases to be merely an institution focused inward or limited by a singular perspective. It becomes a dynamic, Spirit-led movement, equipped to effectively reach the lost, mature believers, discern God's specific will, and pioneer new frontiers for the Kingdom. The evangelist, fully supported, casts the net wide, bringing souls into the community of faith. The prophet, speaking with clarity and boldness, keeps the church aligned with divine truth and purpose, challenging complacency and calling forth holiness. The apostle, with visionary wisdom, lays strong foundations, nurtures leaders, and impels the church outward in its mission to make disciples of all nations.

This is not about seeking a new formula for success, but about returning to the divine pattern laid out in Scripture. A church fully equipped with the manifold gifts of the Spirit, including the often-neglected governmental and missional roles, is a church that will inevitably become more effective, more resilient, and yes, perhaps more "hated for the right reason". It will be hated not for internal squabbles or cultural irrelevance, but because its vibrant life, its selfless love, its uncompromising truth, and its transformative power expose the deficiencies of a world alienated from its Creator. Reclaiming the vitality seen in the early followers of the Galilean Way requires us to be courageous enough to identify where we have drifted and humble enough to make the necessary corrections. By restoring and releasing the full spectrum of ministry gifts, particularly those of the apostle, prophet, and evangelist, and by committing to their material and spiritual support, we take a significant step toward becoming that fierce, world-transforming movement once more—a church truly equipped to manifest the Kingdom of God on earth, as it is in heaven.

CHAPTER 12

A PROPOSED SMALL GROUP MODEL FOR GALILEAN DISCIPLESHIP

To foster a deeper embodiment of the "impious Galilean" spirit, a reimagined small group structure can serve as a powerful catalyst for transformation. This model proposes a four-week rotational cycle, intentionally balancing outward mission, spiritual formation, and internal community care, reflecting the holistic life of the early church.

- **Week 1: Outward-Focused Engagement (Block Party / Open House)** The first week of the cycle would be dedicated to intentional outreach and relationship-building with unbelievers, neighbors, colleagues, school friends, or parents of children's friends. This could take the form of a "block party" or "open house" designed to create a welcoming, low-pressure environment for genuine connection. The goal is to leverage natural relationships, mirroring the early Christians who "gossiped the Gospel" in their daily lives and workplaces. This aligns with pastors' desire for members to embrace evangelism and outreach. The focus is on building bridges and demonstrating Christian love through hospitality and genuine interest in others, rather than a formal religious event.

- **Week 2: Rooted in Scripture and Ancient Principles** The second week would shift to an internal gathering focused on spiritual formation and theological grounding. The group would engage in a Bible study specifically exploring the characteristics of the "impious Galileans" as discussed in this book. Topics would include their radical generosity, open-handedness, and works of service, drawing from scriptural accounts of early Christian communal living and care for the poor. This session would aim to deepen understanding of the theological motivations behind their actions, emphasizing Jesus's "option for the poor" and the "supernatural value" of Christian charity.

- **Week 3: Hands-On Community Service** The third week would be dedicated to tangible acts of service within the broader community. The small group would collectively volunteer at a local food bank, a center for people with disabilities, engage in prison ministry, unhoused ministry, or orphan care. This direct engagement with the marginalized and vulnerable reflects the early church's commitment to practical help and care for those in need, such as widows and strangers. This hands-on service provides an opportunity for members to live out their faith through action, embodying the "option for the poor" and demonstrating Christ's love in tangible ways. It shifts the emphasis from passive learning to active participation in missional living.

- **Week 4: Communal Accountability and Mutual Care** The fourth week would focus on fostering deep communal accountability and mutual care within the small group. This session would provide a safe space for members to share struggles, confess sins, offer encouragement, and provide practical support to one another. Drawing inspiration from Matthew 18:15-17, the emphasis would be on restorative discipline and fostering authentic "siblingship". This internal strengthening is crucial for sustaining the outward mission, ensuring that members are spiritually nourished and relationally supported.

This proposed small group model intentionally interweaves outward mission, theological grounding, practical service, and internal community, providing a concrete framework for developing "impious Galilean" discipleship in the modern church.

CHAPTER 13

THE MINISTRY OF ALL: EVERY BELIEVER AN IMPIOUS GALILEAN IN DAILY LIFE AND WORK

Introduction: Beyond "Church Mice" – The Universal Call to Ministry

Consider this: the average person will spend approximately 90,000 hours at work over their lifetime. That's roughly one-third of your life. If this vast expanse of time and energy is seen as separate from our spiritual lives or our "ministry," we risk missing out on a significant portion of our God-given purpose.

For too long, a subtle (and sometimes not-so-subtle) misconception has permeated parts of the church – the idea that "ministry" is primarily the domain of pastors, missionaries, or a select few highly committed volunteers, the dedicated "church mice" who keep institutional programs running. Dr. John Jackson of William Jessup University critiques this common dysfunction, which often manifests as an 80/20 rule—or even a 10/90 reality—where a small fraction of the congregation carries the vast majority of the ministry load. [15] In his books, such as *Finding Your Place in God's Plan* and *God-Size Your Church*, he argues for what he calls a "full employment policy" in the Body of Christ, a culture where every member is activated for service. The rest, it might be implied, are there to attend, support, and perhaps occasionally participate in a church-organized event. [16]

But what if your "workplace is the primary place of ministry in your life?" This shifts the entire paradigm. It means you are not merely "working to live and living to work". Instead, you are "serving and following God daily, not because of the occasional outreach, missions trip, or service project, but because I am fulfilling and honoring God". As the late Timothy Keller, a prominent voice in the Faith and Work Movement, notes, "in Genesis we see God as a gardener, and in the New Testament we see him as a carpenter. [17] No task is too small a vessel to hold the immense dignity of work given by God". This perspective erases the false dichotomy between sacred and secular work.

The model of the "impious Galileans" we've explored was not one of a small, professionalized clergy leading a passive laity. It was a dynamic, people-driven movement where the faith of ordinary individuals permeated every aspect of their existence, making them a collective force that challenged and changed their world. This all-member engagement, extending far beyond the walls of a church building, is not just a helpful addition; it is critical for the church's vitality, relevance, and its very ability to embody the fierce, transformative love of Christ in a skeptical world, acting as 'the salt of the earth' and 'the light of the world' (Matthew 5:13-16). This is a calling broader and more encompassing than the specialized Levitical model of ancient Israel; it is the New Covenant reality of a "royal priesthood" where every member is empowered for service.

Our Identity in Christ: The Foundation for "Me for We" Ministry

Before we can effectively engage in the "we" of collective ministry, we must be grounded in the "me" of our identity in Christ. But this is not a self-centered "me, me, me" focus;

rather, it is understanding who "me in Christ is" so that we can authentically contribute to the "we". Indeed, an essential understanding is that "if I don't know me than I can't contribute to the we that we are". This journey of self-discovery, however, must be Christ-centered, aiming to make us a "better we".

The apostle Paul underscores this foundational truth: God "chose us in him before the creation of the world to be holy and blameless in his sight". He did not select us based on what we look like, our accomplishments, or our DNA; He chose "you for you". This choice was an act of love, predestining us "for adoption to sonship through Jesus Christ, in accordance with his pleasure and will— to the praise of his glorious grace, which he has freely given us in the One he loves". Our justification comes through faith, not our deeds. John affirms this, stating, "Yet to all who did receive him, to those who believed in his name, he gave the right to become children of God— children born not of natural descent, nor of human decision or a husband's will, but born of God". We are children of God, "for those who are led by the Spirit of God are the children of God". The Spirit we received "does not make you slaves, so that you live in fear again; rather, the Spirit you received brought about your adoption to sonship. And by him we cry, "Abba, Father." The Spirit himself testifies with our spirit that we are God's children". Even before we fully "do me," God welcomes us into the "we" of His family.

This secure identity in Christ, as chosen and beloved children of God, is the wellspring from which all true ministry flows. It frees us from the need for self-promotion or validation through our accomplishments and empowers us to serve others with humility and genuine love, "Do nothing from selfishness or empty conceit, but with humility of mind regard one another as more important than yourselves; do not merely look out for your own personal interests, but also for the interests of others" (Philippians 2:3-4 NASB1995). It is this "me for we" dynamic that allows each individual believer, secure in their unique identity and calling, to contribute powerfully to the collective mission of the Church.

The Dignity of All Work:
Your Vocation as a Sacred Calling

The church must recognize the incredible breadth of talent within its congregation. If we only prepare people for clergy work or give sermons that exclusively deal with the future, we miss the greatest opportunity to equip them for faith and work. The gospel isn't meant to be contained within the church walls; it's meant to be lived out daily in the workplace.

The modern evangelical church often focuses on the "Levite tribe," preparing a small group of people for full-time ministry. But we have a responsibility to equip all eleven other "tribes"—the everyday members called to carry out the mission of the church in their daily lives.

Earlier in this book, we saw that the reputation and identity of the early church were forged by the reputation of its people. The church's witness came directly from the character of its individual members. Over time, the church became a corpus permixtum (a mixed body), where sanctity increasingly resided in the institution itself rather than solely in the radical commitment of individual members. We must return to a model where the church's reputation is built on the daily faithfulness of every person in its congregation, not just its leaders.

The question "What do you do?" often defines us in society, from childhood aspirations to adult interactions. Given that we spend such a significant portion of our lives—those 90,000 hours—at work, it's crucial to understand its potential for purpose. If we don't embrace congregations work as a vital part of our collective calling, we can indeed "miss out on 1/3 of our life purpose, and that's going to affect 'who we are'". Many experience work as a source of stress and anxiety, something to recover from before attempting to engage in family life or church activities where they might be told to "do more!!".

The Faith and Work Movement champions this integration, teaching that all legitimate work has inherent dignity and is a means by which we can glorify God, serve the common good, and participate in God's ongoing creative and redemptive work in the world. [19] Keller further clarifies that working from a "gospel worldview" doesn't mean "constantly speaking about Christian teaching in their work". Rather, the gospel acts like "a set of glasses through which you 'look' at everything else in the world". This worldview shapes our motivations and ethics, so "Christians in business will see profit as only one of several bottom lines; and they will work passionately for any kind of enterprise that serves the common good". This echoes the scriptural call: "So no matter what your task is, work hard. Always do your best as the Lord's servant, not as man's... it is the Lord Christ you are serving" (Colossians 3:23, adapted from source). There is a danger of work becoming merely a means of self-fulfillment, which, as an idea similar to Keller's has warned, "slowly crushes a person" when work is thought of "mainly as a means of self-fulfillment and self-realization". Instead, when "our daily work can be a calling only if it is reconceived as God's assignment to serve others", it becomes a true vocation. It moves followers beyond mere survival or even stability into a life of significance in God's kingdom.

Modern Expressions: Cultivators, Creators, and Redemptive Entrepreneurs

This understanding of work as ministry finds vibrant expression in several contemporary movements. Andy Crouch, [18] in "Culture Making," challenges Christians: "Why aren't we known as cultivators—people who tend and nourish what is best in human culture... Why aren't we known as creators—people who dare to think and do something that has never been thought or done before, something that makes the world more welcoming and thrilling and beautiful?". Instead of merely being "critics, consumers, copiers, condemners of culture", we are called to actively shape it for the better.

Praxis Labs embodies this "cultivator and creator" ethos through its focus on "redemptive entrepreneurship". They are an ecosystem dedicated to equipping and mentoring Christian entrepreneurs who are building ventures—both for-profit and non-profit—that aim to bless people, renew culture, and embody the gospel in tangible ways. Praxis emphasizes a "redemptive imagination," encouraging founders to develop sacrificial strategies, operate their ventures with profound integrity and care for all stakeholders, and create products and services that genuinely contribute to human flourishing.

Similarly, the Faith Driven Entrepreneur Movement (and its counterpart, Faith Driven Investor) started by the very generous Henry Kaestner seeks to activate a global community of individuals who see their entrepreneurial and investment activities as integral to their Christian calling. [20] They provide resources, community, and inspiration to help entrepreneurs build and lead their companies in a way that is fully aligned with their faith.

The grassroots work of leaders like Roy Tinklenberg has also been quietly instrumental. As a silent disrupter and architect of modern faith and work models, his Faith & Work Movement Global began in 2014 by serving Christian employees in Silicon Valley. His efforts, documented at faithandworkmovement.org, have been key in pioneering corporate Christian fellowships and faith-based Employee Resource Groups (ERGs) at major tech companies such as Apple, Cisco, Google, LinkedIn, and Meta, equipping believers to live out their calling in the heart of the global tech industry.

These leaders and movements, from redemptive entrepreneurs at Praxis to the corporate fellowships fostered by Tinklenberg, alongside key contributors like the Theology of Work Project and networks like Made to Flourish [21], all demonstrate that the "impious Galilean" spirit of whole-life discipleship and everyday ministry is very much alive. Believers are increasingly recognizing that their skills, passions, and professional platforms are not separate from their spiritual lives but are God-given assignments to serve others and co-create a more just, beautiful, and flourishing world.

Building the "Tabernacle" Together: Every Contribution Matters

The Old Testament provides a powerful illustration of this all-member participation in the building of the Tabernacle and later, the Temple. When it came time to construct a sanctuary for God to dwell among His people, the call went out broadly: "Tell the Israelites to bring Me an offering. You are to receive My offering from every man whose heart compels him" (Exodus 25:2, adapted from source). The offerings were diverse: "gold, silver, and bronze; blue, purple, and scarlet yarn; fine linen and goat hair; ram skins dyed red and fine leather; acacia wood; oil for lighting; spices for the anointing oil and for the fragrant incense; and onyx and other gemstones to be mounted on the ephod and breast piece". Everyone whose heart was stirred contributed willingly, from their unique resources and abilities, "according to the pattern" God revealed.

Later, for the Temple, "rulers of the fathers' households, and the princes of the tribes of Israel, and the commanders of thousands and of hundreds, with the overseers over the king's work, offered willingly", giving generously of gold, silver, brass, and iron. "Whoever possessed precious stones gave them to the treasury of the house of the LORD". The text emphasizes the joy of the people because "they had offered so willingly, for they made their offering to the LORD with a whole heart, and King David also rejoiced greatly". King David himself contributed his personal treasures "over and above everything I have provided for this holy temple," and then asked, "Now, who is willing to consecrate themselves to the Lord today?".

This principle is profound: God designed the sanctuary, His dwelling place, to be "characteristic of the people of God" because it was built through their collective, willing, and diverse contributions. Each person had a part to play, a unique offering to bring, "according to what God showed them". This wasn't the work of a select few; it was a community effort, driven by devotion and a desire to honor God. Applied to the New Covenant church, this means that the "household of God" (Ephesians 2:19) and its impact in the world are built not by a professional clergy alone, but by the consecrated gifts, talents, resources, and daily work of every single member. Each person, in their unique sphere of influence—their family, workplace, community, artistic endeavors, or business ventures—has a "craft" to offer, a way to contribute to the beauty, strength, and mission of Christ's body on earth.

Conclusion: Unleashing the Fierceness of an All-Member Ministry

The "impious Galilean" spirit that so troubled Emperor Julian was not the product of a few charismatic leaders orchestrating a movement from the top down. It was the organic result of a whole community of people whose lives were so thoroughly transformed by Jesus that their faith naturally overflowed into every interaction, every act of service, every expression of their character. They were all ministers, all witnesses, because their very way of being was a testament to the Kingdom they represented.

Embracing this culture requires a fundamental re-imagining of the role of professional ministry staff. Their primary purpose is not to be the sole providers of ministry, but to become dedicated equippers and trainers of the congregation. The staff are the coaches, and the congregation is the team that plays on the field every day of the week. If this vital work of equipping is neglected, the church is left paralyzed—a body with a head but no limbs to move, touch, or heal the world. Without a fully trained and empowered laity, the church has no hands and feet to be the tangible presence of Christ in the streets, the schools, and the workplaces.

If the contemporary evangelical church is to reclaim this kind of counter-cultural fierceness and avoid irrelevance or mere institutional survival, it must wholeheartedly embrace and actively cultivate an "every member a minister" culture. This means moving decisively beyond any lingering notions of a sacred/secular divide that relegates "real ministry" to a select few or to specific "church activities". It requires equipping and empowering believers to see their daily lives—their work, their relationships, their passions, their entrepreneurial ventures—as the God-ordained arenas for their most significant ministry.

The Faith and Work Movement, Praxis, and the Faith Driven Entrepreneur Movement are not just niche interests; they are vital expressions of what it means for the whole people of God to take seriously their call to be salt and light in every corner of society. When every believer understands their unique identity in Christ and is unleashed to serve God through their specific vocation and daily interactions, the church becomes an unstoppable, "impious" force for good—cultivating beauty, creating solutions, challenging injustice, and drawing others to the compelling love of Christ. This is not just a strategy for church growth; it is the path to becoming the vibrant, world-engaging, Spirit-empowered body that Christ called into being. [22] The question then becomes not "Who will do the ministry?" but, like David, "Who is willing to consecrate themselves to the Lord today in every aspect of their lives?".

PART 4

CONFRONTING MODERN CRISES WITH GALILEAN COMPASSION

CHAPTER 14:

RECLAIMING SACRED SPACE: THE SUNDAY GATHERING OF IMPIOUS GALILEANS

Every church, whether explicitly stated or implicitly understood, operates with a mission—a core purpose often encapsulated in phrases like "love God, love people, love our neighbor," or similar calls to action. These statements articulate our deepest aspirations for impact and transformation. Yet, a critical question often remains unasked: Does our current Sunday service structure and atmosphere truly align with and effectively communicate this intended messaging? Does the experience of our weekly gathering genuinely reflect our desire to love God, love people, and our neighbor?

Sunday is a profound opportunity—a time to show radical hospitality, to forge connections not just with one another, but especially with new people. It's a chance to intentionally bring the lonely into our homes and create a welcoming "table for the visitors," embodying the very essence of the radical "impious Galileans." This chapter is not a critique against any particular church model or style. Rather, it is a call to intentionality: to ensure our Sunday services genuinely embody the impious Galilean spirit when we gather together and reflect the diverse community we aim to serve. We must reconsider *what* we build and *how* we are building it, asking if our investments truly foster genuine connection and spiritual encounter, rather than being controlled by what has "always been" or what we *think* people want. People, fundamentally, desire community with individuals who are radically loving and caring.

I recall attending a "really cool" church in the early 2000s where everyone seemed to wear black and denim, exuding an undeniable sense of being "in." Having come from another service earlier that morning, I arrived in a blue button-down shirt. I did not fit in. (I, of course, went home and changed—kidding!) This experience highlighted a critical truth: a church's culture cannot be so defined by uniformity that others are unable to belong. The same can be said for suits and ties. The intent is not to make *us* comfortable, or to be the "best in show" for an exclusive audience—like a country club where everyone is expected to wear white, for example. True diversity—in age, socioeconomic class, background, race, and even style—is essential. Our gatherings should genuinely look like our people, our region, and our community.

We have explored the profound call for the church to "go" into the world, empowering every believer to be a minister in their daily lives. We have examined how the early "impious Galileans" transformed society not by building impressive edifices or staging grand performances, but by living out a fierce, counter-cultural love that permeated their every interaction. For many, the primary encounter with the church remains the Sunday gathering. This weekly assembly holds immense potential as a gateway for the unchurched, a place for spiritual renewal, and a vital touchpoint for fostering community—a place to live out a fierce, counter-cultural love that permeated their every interaction. However, if our Sunday experience inadvertently mirrors the very consumerist and performance-driven culture we seek to challenge, we risk undermining our mission and alienating those who truly yearn for spiritual depth and authentic connection.

Sundays can become packed with commercials for upcoming campaigns, new building projects, and various church programs, leaving little room for spontaneous spiritual encounter or quiet reflection. The inherent danger here is that the very space intended for spiritual nourishment and divine encounter can feel more like a performance venue or a product showcase, rather than a sanctuary. Our faithful congregants often dedicate 40 or more hours to their jobs and then layer on another ten or more hours a week for church activities and small groups. They come to Sunday services to be filled, equipped, and trained—to receive, not just to be further recruited or entertained.

I remember, after years of building a relationship, inviting my Bay Area banker and her family to my church. I was genuinely excited to show her "our Kid City, our cafe, our stage design"—all the elements we believed made our Sunday experience exceptional. After her visit, she was incredibly gracious, saying, "We felt welcomed, but completely overwhelmed. It was like Disneyland." She explained, "I grew up Buddhist, and my husband Catholic, and we are used to places of reflection, worship, and peace." Her comment was not meant to offend; it was a profound observation. It revealed how, in our earnest efforts to make our experiences "bigger and better" for *us*—our existing congregants—we can unintentionally create environments that are overwhelming, unfamiliar, and even off-putting to those seeking something fundamentally different from the world's clamor. They are not slamming our models, and certainly, some may reach people who need that particular style. However, her perspective underscored a critical point: if our Sunday services feel more like a dazzling production than a sacred encounter, we risk missing the very people we aim to reach.

The "impious Galileans" offer a powerful counter-narrative. They prioritized genuine worship, deep teaching, fervent prayer, and tangible expressions of God's transformative power. Their focus was not on entertaining or marketing, but on encountering Christ and being equipped for their daily mission.

Reclaiming the sacred space of Sunday means reimagining its purpose, aligning it more closely with the ancient Galilean spirit:

- **Every Sunday, An Open Door for Encounter:** Each Sunday is a profound opportunity for someone to "wander in, be invited, and talk about" Jesus. Our services should be designed with this potential encounter at their heart, creating an atmosphere that welcomes and facilitates genuine spiritual exploration, rather than assuming familiarity with our routines or culture. This includes actively putting the lonely in homes and creating a welcoming "table for the visitors," ensuring no one feels overlooked, overwhelmed, or isolated.

- **A Sacred Time for Training, Inspiration, and Worship:** Sunday should be dedicated to training believers for their "go" mission during the week, inspiring them with God's Word, blessing God through unadulterated worship, and celebrating His transformative work in their lives and in the world. Announcements about building projects, campaigns, or future events, while important, can be effectively communicated during the week through digital platforms, newsletters, or dedicated pre/post-service interactions. This frees Sunday for its primary spiritual purpose, ensuring it's not a cascade of "commercials" but a conduit for divine connection.

- **Always Room for Salvation, Baptism, and Prayer:** The core spiritual moments of encountering Christ should always be prioritized. This means consistently providing clear opportunities for individuals to respond to the Gospel message, to celebrate baptisms, and to engage in fervent, corporate prayer. These elements are not incidental; they are central to the sacred purpose of the gathering. Furthermore, moments like communion and baby dedications should be treated with the gravity and sacredness they deserve, providing profound opportunities for congregants and guests alike to witness and participate in deeply meaningful spiritual acts, drawing them closer to God and to the community. Testimonies of life change should be shared not as polished performances, but as authentic, heartfelt accounts of God's work, inspiring faith and demonstrating the Gospel's tangible impact. We should also create space for divine encounters and exceptional healings, allowing the Holy Spirit to move powerfully as the Lord leads, and encouraging congregants to pray for those "poor in spirit or in health."

- **Authenticity Over Performance – Matching the Community:** Sunday is not a performance time for leaders, nor is it a show designed for entertainment. It is a sacred time for people to find Jesus, celebrate Him, and witness others meet for the first time. The focus should remain on the divine encounter and the profound truth of the Gospel, not on human charisma or production spectacle. This is not a "slam" on screens, lights, or smoke; rather, it is a call to match the community in which the church is embedded. If the target audience—whether youth, young adults, or others—is accustomed to light shows and dynamic presentations, by all means, incorporate those elements! The point is increasing *genuine expression* and *connection to meet God* is the true aim. This means reflecting the diversity of the community in all ways – in the praise, the tone of communication, and the overall energy of the gathering. The message delivered should also reflect the community's needs and context. Tools like Gloo.com can be invaluable in learning the region's spiritual learning style, enabling the church to tailor its approach to genuinely connect with the hearts and minds of the people it serves.

- **Meeting Real Community Needs:** Meeting real community needs, as "impious Galileans," involves knowing our community—exegeting our city's past and present. This includes understanding crucial data such as divorce rates, domestic abuse rates, abortion numbers, prevalence of diseases, homelessness statistics, and mental health information. Being equipped and prayerful allows you to meet these needs, as the Lord leads, offers authentic relevance. God encourages us to ask for divine encounters, words, and scripture to meet every person in the room, even a prophetic word if the Lord uses us for this. If you ever feel stuck or fall into routine you can pray, as I do when I become stagnant or fall into routine: "Lord, renew the joy of my salvation and renew a right spirit within me" (Psalm 51:10), ensuring your witness flows from a deeply connected and authentic place.

When our Sunday gatherings remain a place of reflection, peace, and transformative power that resonates deeply with a world longing for the authentic presence of Jesus they become a wellspring that fuels the "go congregation" throughout the week. It empower "Impious Galileans" to live out their faith authentically, making the church's daily witness in the community the most compelling demonstration of Christ's fierce and tender love.

CHAPTER 15

THE SILENT EXODUS: WHY A GENERATION IS ADRIFT AND THE GALILEAN CALL HOME

Introduction: The Vanishing Generation

The landscape of faith in many Western societies is undergoing a seismic shift, most notably marked by what can be described as a "silent exodus"—the steady and often quiet departure of younger generations from traditional church affiliation and, for some, from Christian faith altogether. This is not a fringe phenomenon but a well-documented trend that carries profound implications for the future vitality and mission of the church.

Statistics from respected research organizations paint a clear, and for many, alarming picture. For example, the Pew Research Center has consistently tracked the rise of the "nones"—those who identify as religiously unaffiliated (atheist, agnostic, or "nothing in particular"). Their findings indicate that this group is significantly larger among younger adults (Millennials and Gen Z) compared to older generations. A 2021 Pew report revealed that about three in ten U.S. adults are now "nones," a figure that has grown substantially in recent decades (Pew Research Center, "About three-in-ten U.S. adults are now religiously unaffiliated," 2021). Similarly, Barna Group research frequently highlights the challenges churches face in retaining and engaging young adults, with many who grew up in the church disengaging during their late teens and twenties (Barna Group data). Studies focusing specifically on Gen Z (those born after 1996) often describe them as the least religious generation on record in terms of traditional metrics like church attendance and self-identification with a particular faith. For instance, analyses of data like the American National Family Life Survey have shown a substantial portion of Gen Z never or rarely attend religious services.

This vanishing act from the pews and, in some cases, from the foundational tenets of faith, is not something to be dismissed with simplistic explanations or ignored out of discomfort. It is a clarion call for the church to engage in deep introspection and courageous re-evaluation. Why are so many young people adrift? What are they seeking that they are not finding within the current expressions of institutional Christianity? And crucially, does the ancient, yet ever-radical, way of the "impious Galileans" offer a path toward a more authentic, compelling, and ultimately, life-giving expression of faith that might call a wandering generation home? This chapter will explore the reasons behind this exodus and propose that the core characteristics of the early church provide a timeless blueprint for re-engagement.

Echoes in the Emptiness: Reasons for Disaffiliation

Understanding why young people are drifting from the church requires listening carefully to their "echoes in the emptiness"—the often complex and varied reasons behind their disengagement. Research from institutions like Barna, Pew, and the Springtide Research Institute [23] consistently points to several recurring themes:

- **Perceived Hypocrisy and Judgment:** Many young people report a disconnect between the stated ideals of Christianity and the observed behavior of Christians or churches. They are highly attuned to perceived hypocrisy, judgmental attitudes, and a lack of genuine compassion, which can be deeply alienating (Barna Group findings; Pew Research data).

■ **The Science-Faith Divide and Intellectual Obstacles:** For some, the perceived conflict between science and faith, or a lack of intellectually satisfying answers to their challenging questions about God, suffering, and the Bible, creates a significant barrier. Churches that avoid tough questions or offer simplistic answers may fail to engage those who are wrestling with these issues (Barna Group findings).

■ **Stance on Social Issues:** The church's positions on various contemporary social issues, particularly those related to sexuality, gender, and social justice, are often cited as major points of divergence for younger generations who may hold more progressive views or prioritize inclusivity differently (Pew Research data; Barna Group findings).

■ **Negative Personal Experiences:** Traumatic or negative experiences within a church context—such as spiritual abuse, unhealthy leadership dynamics, or feeling unseen and unvalued—can lead to a profound and lasting disaffiliation.

■ **Perceived Irrelevance:** A significant number simply drift away because they do not see the church or organized religion as relevant to their daily lives, their struggles, or the pressing problems of the world. If faith doesn't connect with their lived reality or offer meaningful ways to engage with the world, it can easily be sidelined.

■ **Longing for Authenticity and Genuine Community:** Many young people are seeking authentic relationships and a genuine sense of belonging. Springtide Research Institute, for example, notes that while young people may be leaving institutions, many are still highly spiritual and are actively seeking communities where they can be their authentic selves and explore life's big questions (Springtide Research Institute findings). [23] If churches are perceived as superficial, overly programmed, or lacking in deep, meaningful connections, they will fail to meet this fundamental human need.

- **Moral and Political Disagreements:** For some, the entanglement of certain expressions of Christianity with specific political ideologies, partisan loyalties, or what is perceived as a "political church" focused on power rather than service, can be a significant reason for stepping away. When the church is seen as primarily a political block, or when its public witness is characterized more by culture-warring and condemnation than by Christ-like love and compassion, it can alienate those who long for a faith that transcends and critiques all political systems with a prophetic, Kingdom-centered voice.

These reasons are not exhaustive, and individuals often have a combination of factors influencing their journey away from the church. However, these recurring themes provide crucial insights into the areas where the contemporary church is often failing to connect with or retain its younger members. Addressing this "silent exodus" requires more than new programs or trendier worship styles; it demands a fundamental re-examination of the church's core character, mission, and how it embodies the love and truth of Christ in the world.

The Galilean Contrast: A Church Worth Believing In?

If the prevailing expressions of church often leave young people feeling empty, judged, or unconvinced, what did the early "impious Galileans" offer that proved so compelling, even in a hostile environment? The contrast is stark and instructive. These early believers lived under the shadow of the Roman Empire—a pagan, often oppressive, and deeply suspicious regime. They possessed no political power, had no worldly status to leverage, and certainly did not seek to impose their faith through imperial decree or partisan maneuvering. Their influence, the very thing that made them "hated for the right reason" and simultaneously drew thousands into their fold, stemmed not from political activism, riots, protests, or aggressive attacks on their cultural or religious opponents, but from the sheer, undeniable power of their transformed lives and their counter-cultural community.

Consider these Galilean characteristics as direct responses to the modern "echoes in the emptiness":

- **Authenticity and Integrity over Hypocrisy:** The early Christians were known for their moral seriousness and the consistency between their beliefs and actions. While not perfect, their earnest pursuit of holiness and their systems of mutual accountability created a culture of integrity that stood in sharp contrast to both the licentiousness of pagan society and any internal hypocrisy. This authenticity is a powerful magnet for a generation weary of duplicity.

- **Radical, Universal Charity over Judgment:** Julian the Apostate himself lamented that the "impious Galileans support not only their own poor but ours as well". This indiscriminate, sacrificial love and care for all, regardless of belief or social standing, was their most potent apologetic. It was a tangible demonstration of God's love that disarmed critics and met genuine human needs, offering a compelling alternative to a spirit of judgment or condemnation.

- **Deep, Inclusive Community over Superficiality:** The early church was a true "siblingship," a close-knit family that shared life and resources. In a fragmented and hierarchical world, this radical community offered profound belonging and mutual support. For young people today craving genuine connection beyond the superficiality of social media or a "country club mentality" within some churches, this kind of authentic, life-sharing community is deeply appealing.

- **A Faith Engaging Real-World Issues over Perceived Irrelevance:** The Galileans' faith was not an abstract set of doctrines confined to private devotion; it directly addressed the pressing social issues of their day—poverty, care for the sick and widowed, burial of the dead, infanticide. They were seen as a "force for good" not because they lobbied Caesar for policy changes, but because they *were* the change, actively creating a society within a society that reflected the values of God's Kingdom. This tangible relevance speaks volumes to those who want to see faith make a real difference in the world.

- **Intellectual Engagement and Reasoned Defense over Simplistic Answers:** While characterized by "ordinary" people, the early church also engaged in "apologetics," providing a "reasoned defense" of their faith tailored to their audiences. They were not afraid of questions and sought to articulate their hope with clarity and conviction, a vital approach for engaging intellectually curious young minds.

- **A Kingdom Not of This World, Yet Transforming This World:** Critically, the early Christians understood their primary allegiance was to Christ and His Kingdom, not to Rome or any earthly power. This allowed them to live as good citizens where possible but also to critique and resist (often passively, through non-conformity) the idolatries and injustices of the empire. Their power was spiritual and moral, not political in the partisan sense. They thrived through their witness and actions, demonstrating a better way of life rather than trying to seize the levers of worldly power to enforce their views. This "third way" offers a powerful model for a church seeking to influence culture without being co-opted or corrupted by partisan politics.

The "impious Galilean" church was, in essence, a community so radically transformed by the love of Christ that it could not help but live differently. It was this lived difference—their love, their justice, their community, their integrity, their unwavering hope even in the face of persecution—that made them a compelling witness. This is the kind of church, we contend, that can begin to call a drifting generation home.

Re-imagining Engagement: Pathways for a Modern Galilean Church

If the "Galilean contrast" offers a compelling model, how can the contemporary church practically embody these principles to re-engage a drifting generation and, more broadly, to become a more authentic and impactful presence in the world? It requires a conscious "re-imagining" of what engagement truly means, shifting from paradigms that may inadvertently alienate to approaches that reflect the counter-cultural wisdom of the early believers.

- **Prioritize Embodied Witness over Partisan Politics:** As we've noted, the early "impious Galileans" transformed their world not by seizing political power or engaging in adversarial partisan battles, but through the compelling witness of their lives and actions. A modern Galilean church must consciously disentangle itself from being perceived as an arm of any specific political party. Its primary mode of influence should be its Christ-like service, its pursuit of justice rooted in biblical principles (not partisan agendas), and the transformed lives of its people. This means focusing energy on tangible acts of love, community building, and caring for the vulnerable, rather than primarily on political activism or culture-warring as a means of societal change. This approach offers a more universally compelling witness, especially to young people wary of political polarization.

- **Cultivate Authentic Community and Deep Belonging:** Many young people are not necessarily rejecting God, but rather a version of "church" that feels superficial, judgmental, or lacking in genuine connection. A Galilean church actively fosters deep, authentic relationships— what the early church called *koinonia* or "siblingship". This involves creating spaces (beyond just Sunday services) for vulnerability, mutual support, shared life, and intergenerational mentorship in the spirit of "hānai". When the church becomes a true spiritual family where people are known, loved, and belong, it addresses one of the deepest longings of the human heart, particularly for an isolated generation.

- **Foster Open Dialogue and Intellectual Honesty:** Instead of shying away from difficult questions about faith, science, suffering, or biblical interpretation, a Galilean church creates safe environments for honest exploration and doubt. It values intellectual integrity and equips its members to think critically and articulate their faith thoughtfully. This approach respects the intelligence of young people and demonstrates that Christianity is a robust worldview capable of engaging with complex issues.

- **Champion Tangible Love, Service, and Justice:** The early church's credibility was profoundly linked to its radical care for the poor, the sick, and the marginalized. A modern Galilean church must be known more for what it *does* in love than what it says in judgment. This means actively identifying and addressing needs within its local community, partnering with others for the common good, and being a consistent voice and agent for biblical justice. When young people see the church making a tangible positive difference in people's lives and in society, its message gains credibility. This looks like:

  - Creating innovative solutions for homelessness, such as Community First! Village in Austin, Texas, which provides affordable, permanent housing and a supportive community for men and women coming out of chronic homelessness. (MLF.org) [28]

- Meeting critical needs with dignity and offering pathways to self-sufficiency, as exemplified by Project WeHOPE [26] in East Palo Alto, California. Led by Pastor Paul Bains, this organization provides emergency and transitional housing, and their "Dignity on Wheels" mobile hygiene outreach offers showers and laundry services to the unhoused, alongside broader efforts in job training and forming foundations for a better future. (WeHOPE.org) [26]

- Bringing essential services directly to under-served children and families in their own neighborhoods. Organizations like Mobilize Love, co-founded by Christian Huang, deploy fleets of trucks that offer services like wellness checks, dental care, academic support, and even a mobile general store for kids in vulnerable communities, demonstrating practical love and support right where people are. (MobilizeLove.org) [25]

- Combating modern-day slavery, an effort championed by organizations like Hope for Justice, which works globally from its UK origins to prevent human trafficking, rescue victims, restore lives, and reform society. The work of individuals like Tim Nelson, co-founder of the National Trafficking Sheltered Alliance and CEO of Hope for Justice, further underscores the critical role of dedicated efforts in this arena, focusing on bringing restorative care to survivors and improving victim identification. (HopeForJustice.org) [24]

- Mobilizing local churches to meet the specific needs of children and families in crisis right in their own communities. CarePortal [27], an initiative with leaders like Adrien Lewis, uses a technology platform to connect local child welfare workers with nearby churches that can respond to the real-time needs of vulnerable families, from providing beds and clothing to offering relational support. (CarePortal.org) [27]

- Fostering compassion and care at the most grass-roots levels, even in schools. Student-led initiatives like the Oasis campus club at Kaiser High School in Honolulu, which my son and daughters help lead, aim to cultivate an environment of love, compassion, and care among students, demonstrating how the impulse to serve and support others can take root early and make a difference in everyday environments. While individual school clubs may vary, the existence of thousands of such faith-motivated, service-oriented student groups across the nation points to a widespread desire among young people to live out their values practically.

These diverse examples, from large-scale organizations to local community efforts, illustrate the "impious Galilean" spirit in action—Christians and church communities rolling up their sleeves to bring tangible hope and healing to a hurting world. When the church is seen as a credible force for good, actively addressing suffering and injustice, its appeal, especially to a generation hungry for authenticity and impact, grows immeasurably.

- **Empower Young People in Meaningful Ministry and Leadership:** Rather than seeing youth as merely a demographic to be programmed for or retained, a Galilean church recognizes them as vital members of the body with unique gifts and perspectives. This involves creating genuine opportunities for them to lead, serve, and shape the church's mission in meaningful ways, not just in token roles. Mentoring them into leadership and valuing their contributions fosters a sense of ownership and purpose.

- **Address Core Human Longings: Identity, Purpose, and Hope:** In a world of shifting identities and existential anxieties, the Gospel offers profound answers to the deepest human questions: Who am I? Why am I here? Where am I going? A Galilean church clearly and compellingly articulates this message of hope, showing how a relationship with Christ provides a secure identity, an ultimate purpose, and an unshakable hope that transcends circumstances. This involves discipling people in their true identity as beloved children of God, free from the pressures of performance or societal validation.

By focusing on these pathways, the church moves from being perceived as an out-of-touch institution to becoming a dynamic, life-giving community that embodies the love, truth, and justice of Christ. This kind of engagement, rooted in the spirit of the "impious Galileans," has the potential not only to re-engage those who have drifted but also to make the church a compelling force for good in a world desperately in need of hope and healing.

Conclusion: The Unchanging Appeal of a Fierce, Loving Christ Manifested Through His People

The silent exodus of a generation from the halls of the church is more than a statistical trend; it is a profound spiritual and existential challenge that calls for an equally profound response. We have seen the sobering data on disaffiliation and explored the complex tapestry of reasons—from perceived hypocrisy and political entanglement to a longing for intellectual honesty, authentic community, and tangible relevance. These are not frivolous complaints; they are the earnest cries of hearts seeking something more, something real, something that truly speaks to the deepest questions and longings of their lives.

In the face of this modern crisis, the ancient way of the "impious Galileans" emerges not as a relic of the past, but as a surprisingly relevant and potent blueprint for the future. Theirs was a faith lived out under the shadow of an often-hostile empire, yet it thrived not through political maneuvering, cultural accommodation, or coercive power, but through the compelling witness of lives radically transformed by love. Their integrity, their sacrificial care for all, their deep and inclusive community, and their courageous engagement with the suffering of their world stood in stark contrast to the prevailing norms, making their message undeniable. They were, in essence, a church worth believing in because their actions consistently validated their words.

Re-imagining engagement today through a Galilean lens means a conscious shift: prioritizing embodied witness over partisan strife, cultivating deep belonging over superficial programs, championing tangible acts of love and justice exemplified by movements and local efforts from Community First! Village [28] to Project WeHOPE [26], Mobilize Love [25], Hope for Justice [24], CarePortal [27], and even student-led compassion like the Oasis clubs. It means fostering environments of open dialogue, empowering every member, and consistently pointing to the secure identity, profound purpose, and unwavering hope found in Christ.

This is not a call for the church to become "cool" or to chase fleeting cultural trends. It is a call to return to something far more ancient and far more powerful: the authentic, counter-cultural, community-centric, and fiercely loving way of Jesus as embodied by His earliest followers. The hunger for truth, for belonging, for purpose, and for a faith that makes a tangible difference in the world remains deeply embedded in the human heart, especially among the young. The unchanging appeal of Christ, when manifested authentically and sacrificially through His people, still has the power to cut through the noise of a cynical world and call a wandering generation home. The path of the "impious Galilean" is not an easy one, but it is a path modeled by Christ Himself, and it may well be the most crucial pathway for the church to not only survive but to thrive with fierce, transformative impact in the challenging days ahead.

CHAPTER 16

AN EPIDEMIC OF DESPAIR: THE GALILEAN RESPONSE TO A WORLD OVERWHELMED BY ANXIETY, DEPRESSION, AND LONELINESS

Introduction: The Inner Pandemic

Beyond the visible crises that often capture headlines, a quieter, yet profoundly devastating, pandemic is sweeping across modern society: an epidemic of despair. We live in an age marked by unprecedented technological advancement and material comfort for many, yet also by skyrocketing rates of anxiety, depression, suicidal ideation, and pervasive loneliness. These are not abstract concerns; they are the lived realities of millions, cutting across age, gender, and socioeconomic strata.

Statistics paint a sobering picture. Even before the global upheavals of recent years, the National Institute of Mental Health (NIMH) reported that approximately one in five U.S. adults lived with a mental illness (NIMH data). The Centers for Disease Control and Prevention (CDC) has noted significant increases in reported symptoms of anxiety and depressive disorders, particularly among younger adults (CDC data). The U.S. Surgeon General has issued advisories spotlighting a critical youth mental health crisis, indicating that mental health challenges were already the leading cause of disability and poor life outcomes in young people, with up to 20% of children aged 3-17 experiencing a mental, emotional, developmental, or behavioral disorder (U.S. Surgeon General's Advisory). Tragically, suicide remains a leading cause of death for those aged 10-34 in the United States, according to CDC data. Globally, the World Health Organization (WHO) identifies depression as a leading cause of disability worldwide, with anxiety disorders also rampant (WHO data). Compounding this is an epidemic of loneliness. Studies like Cigna's Loneliness Index and research from Harvard's "Making Caring Common" project have revealed that a significant majority of adults, with Gen Z and Millennials often reporting the highest levels, feel profoundly lonely or socially isolated (Cigna Loneliness Index; Harvard research). This "inner pandemic" of emotional and mental anguish constitutes a deep "poverty of spirit" that pervades our communities. For a church aspiring to reclaim the fierce, compassionate spirit of the "impious Galileans," these realities cannot be ignored. They demand a response that goes beyond superficial solutions, one that addresses the very core of human brokenness.

The Neglected Soul: Insights from Dallas Willard and John Ortberg

What lies at the heart of this widespread despair? While societal, economic, and physiological factors play a role, theologians and spiritual thinkers like the late Dallas Willard and John Ortberg point to a deeper, often overlooked dimension: the state of the human soul. Willard frequently described the soul (also referred to biblically as the "heart" or "spirit") as the very essence of the human person—the command center of our will, the shaper of our thoughts, the wellspring of our emotions, and the crucible of our character. It is, as Proverbs 4:23 suggests, "the wellspring of life," determining the trajectory and quality of our existence and actions. [29] The health of this inner core is paramount.

John Ortberg, building on Willard's teachings in his book *Soul Keeping*, poignantly argues that "the soul is the deepest part of you, and its health is the most important thing in your existence". [30] He describes the common modern condition of a soul that is hurried, fragmented, overstimulated, and disconnected—a "sick soul" whose symptoms manifest as anxiety, emptiness, irritability, an inability to truly love, and a general sense of meaninglessness. Ortberg emphasizes that every soul needs a "keeper". While God is the ultimate keeper, we bear a responsibility to intentionally care for our own souls in partnership with Him.

For Willard, the path to a healthy soul lies in "spiritual formation"—the intentional process through which our inner world, our spirit and will, is progressively conformed to the image of Jesus Christ. This is not an automatic outcome of religious belief but a journey requiring conscious effort, engagement with God's grace, and the practice of spiritual disciplines. In *The Spirit of the Disciplines*, Willard reframes these disciplines (such as solitude, silence, prayer, fasting, study, simplicity, service, and fellowship) not as means of earning salvation or God's favor, nor as burdensome duties, but as "means of grace". They are intelligently chosen activities through which we "get in the way of grace," arranging our lives to better receive God's transformative power (Willard, *The Spirit of the Disciplines*). He often employed a "VIM" model for this transformation: a clear Vision of Christlike life, a resolute Intention to pursue it, and the application of appropriate Means (disciplines and reliance on grace) to achieve it (Willard, conceptual model). The goal, as articulated in *Renovation of the Heart*, is a thorough reordering and healing of our inner being, so that our thoughts, feelings, habits, and even our bodies increasingly reflect the wholeness and love of Jesus.

If the modern epidemic of despair is, at least in part, a crisis of neglected, disordered, and unhealthy souls, then any meaningful response from the church must include a robust understanding and practice of "soul keeping" and spiritual formation. This is not a retreat from the world's problems, but the cultivation of the inner resilience, wisdom, and Christ-like character necessary to engage those problems redemptively.

The Early Church as a Therapeutic Community

While the early Christians did not possess our modern psychological vocabulary, the communities they formed were, in many ways, profoundly therapeutic. The "impious Galileans," in their radical departure from prevailing social norms, cultivated an environment that inherently ministered to the deep needs of the human soul. Their distinctiveness was not just in their doctrines or their outward acts of charity, but in the very fabric of their shared life, which offered powerful antidotes to the despair, isolation, and meaninglessness common in their own era—and strikingly similar to our own.

Consider the core characteristics we've observed:

- **Profound Belonging and Acceptance ("Siblingship"):** In a rigidly hierarchical Roman world, rife with social divisions, the early church offered a radical vision of community where distinctions of ethnicity, social class, and gender were softened in Christ (Galatians 3:28). This created a deep sense of "siblingship" and belonging that was counter-cultural. For individuals who were marginalized, lonely, or seeking a place of genuine acceptance, this was a powerful draw. This loving inclusion was a balm to souls wounded by societal rejection or familial brokenness.

- **Shared Life, Mutual Support, and Burden-Bearing:** The early believers didn't just meet once a week; they were deeply involved in each other's lives. They shared meals, resources (Acts 2:44-45, Acts 4:32-35), and actively bore one another's burdens (Galatians 6:2). This practical, day-to-day support system provided an emotional and spiritual safety net, crucial for navigating life's hardships. Knowing you were not alone in your struggles, that others would genuinely care for and assist you, fostered resilience and emotional well-being.

- **A Sense of Purpose and Hope Rooted in the Gospel:** The Christian message offered a compelling narrative of hope, redemption, and ultimate meaning that stood in stark contrast to the often fatalistic or cynical worldviews of the time. This eschatological hope, combined with the present reality of God's Kingdom breaking in, gave believers a profound sense of purpose that transcended their personal circumstances. This purposefulness is a key ingredient for mental and emotional health, combating the despair that often accompanies a perceived lack of meaning.

- **Practices that Fostered Spiritual and Emotional Well-being:** The regular rhythms of early Christian life included practices that we now recognize as conducive to soul health. Communal prayer, the singing of psalms and hymns, the reading and meditation on Scripture, shared meals (including the Eucharist/Love Feast), and even intentional practices like fasting, were not merely religious duties but formative activities that shaped their inner lives. These practices provided avenues for expressing grief and joy, finding comfort, reinforcing communal bonds, and encountering God – all vital for a healthy soul.

- **Counter-Cultural Ethics and a Call to Transformation:** The call to live a life of holiness, distinct from the prevailing vices of the surrounding culture (as noted by Pliny and Julian regarding their moral sobriety), provided a clear moral compass and a pathway for personal growth and transformation. This pursuit of virtue, within a supportive community, could foster a strong sense of identity and self-respect, contributing positively to one's inner state.

The "impious Galileans" created communities where souls could genuinely thrive, not because they had formal "mental health programs," but because their entire way of life—centered on love, shared existence, mutual accountability, and a vibrant relationship with God—was inherently restorative and life-giving. Their radical commitment to one another and to the teachings of Jesus naturally cultivated an environment where loneliness was diminished, anxiety could be shared and alleviated, and a deep sense of belonging and purpose could flourish. This ancient model offers profound wisdom for a modern church seeking to minister to an epidemic of despair. It reminds us that true "soul care" is often less about specific programs and more about cultivating a specific kind of community—one that embodies the fierce, compassionate, and healing love of Christ.

Becoming a Sanctuary for the Hurting: Practical Steps for a Galilean Church Today

If the contemporary church is to emulate the "impious Galileans" by becoming a genuine force for healing in a world gripped by an epidemic of despair, it must intentionally cultivate environments and practices that minister to the whole person, particularly the wounded soul. This involves more than simply acknowledging the problem; it requires concrete, compassionate action rooted in the principles of "soul keeping" and the example of the early Christian community.

This principle of meeting the actual, pressing needs of a community is powerfully illustrated by the work of Pastor Tyler Scott and Community Presbyterian Church (CPC) in Danville, California. In their affluent area of the San Ramon Valley, the most profound poverty wasn't necessarily a lack of food or physical shelter, but a deep poverty of spirit manifesting as anxiety, depression, and relational brokenness. A traditional soup kitchen might have missed the community's deepest ache. Recognizing this, CPC took a courageous and context-specific 'impious Galilean' step. Instead of launching a program that fit a generic mold of charity, they identified the real need and invested in creating the Community Presbyterian Counseling Center (CPCC). This professional, faith-based center provides clinical therapy and mental health services to the community, directly addressing the epidemic of despair. This is a crucial modern lesson: being a Galilean church doesn't always mean financial aid to the materially poor; it means discerning the unique 'poverty' of one's specific mission field and providing a tangible, excellent, and Christ-centered response.

Here are some practical steps for becoming a sanctuary for the hurting:

- **Integrate "Soul Care" into the Core of Church Life:**

  - **Teaching and Modeling Spiritual Disciplines:** Following the wisdom of Dallas Willard and John Ortberg, churches can actively teach on the nature of the soul and the importance of its care. This includes providing practical guidance on engaging with spiritual disciplines (solitude, silence, prayer, scripture meditation, simplicity, fasting, fellowship, service) not as legalistic duties, but as life-giving "means of grace" that help individuals connect with God and foster inner transformation (Willard, *The Spirit of the Disciplines*; Ortberg, *Soul Keeping*). Willard's VIM (Vision, Intention, Means) model can be a helpful framework for discipleship programs aimed at genuine heart renovation.

  - **Preaching and Worship that Glorifies God:** Sermons can address the realities of anxiety, depression, and loneliness with honesty and biblical hope, pointing to Christ as the ultimate healer of souls. Preaching deeply rooted in scripture and not hype culture filled with quips and tips. Worship services, in turn, should be designed as spaces for genuine encounter with God, fostering not just instruction or performance, but a reckless surrender to, and admiration of, God's power, His faithful works throughout all time—hours, days, weeks, months, and years—and ultimately, His profound love and inherent worthiness of praise simply because He is God. Such authentic, God-centered worship naturally becomes a source of deep solace, a safe space for lament, and a wellspring of hope that powerfully resonates with hurting hearts.

- **Establish a Culture of Foundational Trust and Professionalism:**

  - **Paramount Safety and Confidentiality:** The church *must* be a safe place. This requires establishing and rigorously upholding clear policies on confidentiality. The tendency for prayer requests about individuals' struggles to devolve into gossip, however unintentional, is deeply damaging and renders the church unsafe for those most in need of care.

  - **Professional Ethics in Pastoral Care:** Church staff and key ministry leaders should be trained in ethical conduct regarding sensitive personal information. A culture of professionalism, where trust is paramount and discretion is absolute, is non-negotiable for a church that claims to be a sanctuary. This professionalism doesn't negate warmth or love but undergirds it with integrity.

- **Create Safe and Authentically Vulnerable Communities:**

  - **Small Groups Focused on Authentic Connection:** Building on a foundation of trust, small groups can become places for genuine sharing of struggles, mutual support, and prayer for inner healing, moving beyond superficial interactions. The goal is to create "no-shame zones" where people feel safe to be honest about their inner lives without fear of judgment or their confidences being broken.

  - **Emphasize Hospitality and Inclusive Welcome:** The radical acceptance found in early Christian communities needs to be replicated. Churches can actively work to ensure that newcomers and those on the margins feel genuinely welcomed, seen, and valued, combating the isolation that fuels despair.

- **Foster Generational Connectivity and Reciprocal Mentorship (The Spirit of "Hānai"):**

  - **Intergenerational Relationships:** Actively create opportunities for meaningful connections between different generations within the church. This can counter societal fragmentation and provide diverse perspectives and support.

  - **Mentoring and Discipleship:** Encourage formal and informal mentoring relationships where older generations can "hānai" (a Hawaiian term for an informal fostering, nurturing, or adopting relationship) younger members—acting as uncles, aunties, spiritual grandparents, or older siblings. This involves listening, teaching, sharing life wisdom, and providing guidance.

  - **Reciprocal Learning & Accountability:** These relationships should be reciprocal, with younger generations also sharing their insights and experiences. Within these safe, "hānai"-like connections, individuals can more readily admit struggles, share sins, and enlist accountability, knowing they are in a nurturing and trustworthy environment.

- **Equip for Compassionate Ministry:**

  - **Mental Health Awareness and Basic Training:** Pastors, staff, and lay leaders can benefit immensely from basic mental health first aid training or workshops on mental health awareness. This helps them recognize signs of distress, respond with empathy, and know when and how to guide someone towards professional help, always maintaining ethical boundaries.

- **Develop a Culture of Compassionate Listening:** Training in active, non-judgmental listening skills for small group leaders and care teams can make a significant difference. Often, hurting individuals first need someone to simply listen to their pain without offering quick fixes or theological platitudes.

- **Reduce Stigma and Normalize Conversations about Mental Health:**

  - **Openly Address Mental Health from the Pulpit and in Teaching:** When leaders speak openly and compassionately about mental health struggles, it helps to reduce the shame and stigma that often prevent people from seeking help within the church.

  - **Share Testimonies of Healing and Hope:** Hearing stories from others who have navigated mental health challenges within a faith context can be incredibly encouraging and destigmatizing.

- **Actively Partner with and Enlist Professional Care:**

  - **Build Bridges with Professionals:** Churches should actively enlist the help of and build collaborative relationships with Christian doctors, psychologists, therapists, and other mental health professionals. This might involve inviting them to give seminars, consulting with them on church policies, or having them as part of a trusted referral network.

  - **Clear Referral Pathways:** Knowing when a situation requires professional intervention beyond the church's pastoral care capacity is crucial. Having established, trusted pathways for referral ensures individuals receive the appropriate level of care.

- **Champion Loving Relationships and Authentic Connection:** As seen with the "impious Galileans," the power of genuine, loving relationships is immense. Every initiative, from welcoming teams to small groups to service projects, should be infused with the goal of fostering authentic human connection, which is a powerful antidote to loneliness and a key component of a healthy soul. The spirit of "hānai" – of nurturing, adopting, and investing deeply in one another – should permeate the church culture.

By intentionally implementing such practices, a church begins to embody the spirit of the "impious Galileans"—not just as a place of correct doctrine or charitable deeds, but as a true sanctuary, a community deeply committed to the healing and flourishing of every soul God brings through its doors or into its sphere of influence. This kind of church becomes a beacon of hope, demonstrating in tangible ways the compassionate heart of Christ.

Conclusion: The Impious Galilean – A Healer of Souls, Not Just a Dispenser of Doctrine

The staggering statistics of anxiety, depression, loneliness, and other forms of inner turmoil paint a clear picture: modern society is grappling with a profound crisis of the soul. In such a landscape, the church is called to be far more than a dispenser of doctrine or a curator of religious services. It is summoned, much like the "impious Galileans" of old, to be a tangible manifestation of God's healing and restorative presence in a broken world. The early Christians earned their counter-cultural reputation not only through their unwavering faith and ethical distinctiveness but also through their radical compassion and the transformative power of their communal life, which inherently nurtured the well-being of its members.

As we have explored, insights from thinkers like Dallas Willard and John Ortberg on "soul keeping" and spiritual formation provide a vital framework for understanding how this inner healing and transformation can be intentionally cultivated. Their emphasis on the care of the soul—that deepest part of our being—and the intelligent use of spiritual disciplines as means of grace, offers a path beyond superficial religiosity to deep, Christ-like character formation. This is not a retreat into navel-gazing piety, but the essential groundwork for building resilient individuals and, consequently, a resilient and impactful church.

The modern church, by embracing its role as a sanctuary for the hurting—a place of profound trust, authentic community, intergenerational connection in the spirit of "hānai," compassionate listening, and wise partnership with professional care—can begin to address the "inner pandemic" with the same fierce love the Galileans applied to the outward needs they encountered. This involves more than adding new programs; it requires a cultural shift towards prioritizing the holistic well-being of every individual, fostering environments where souls are safe, seen, and skillfully tended.

To be "impious Galileans" in the 21st century means recognizing that the Gospel speaks to every dimension of human suffering, including the hidden anguish of the mind and spirit. When the church becomes known as a community where broken souls find healing, where the lonely find true belonging, where the anxious find peace, and where the despairing find hope, it will once again demonstrate a relevance and power that the world cannot ignore. This is the path to not only addressing an epidemic of despair but also to revitalizing the church's own soul, making it a radiant beacon of Christ's comprehensive love and a true healer of souls in a world desperate for wholeness.

CHAPTER 17

MENDING THE TORN FABRIC: A GALILEAN APPROACH TO RELATIONAL BROKENNESS, ABUSE, AND IDENTITY

Introduction: A World of Fractured Connections and Wounded Identities

Beyond the pervasive anxiety and depression explored previously, modern society is also deeply scarred by fractured relationships, the devastating impact of abuse, and widespread confusion surrounding identity and self-worth. These are not isolated incidents but systemic wounds in the fabric of our communities, affecting millions and contributing to the broader sense of unease and brokenness.

Consider the landscape:

- **Relational Brokenness:** Divorce rates, while having seen some fluctuations, remain a significant reality, leaving a trail of emotional pain for spouses and children, and reshaping family structures (CDC data; American Psychological Association findings). Beyond divorce, many experience deep loneliness even within families, or the slow erosion of meaningful friendships in a fast-paced, digitally mediated world.

- **The Scourge of Abuse:** The statistics on abuse are horrifying and demand urgent attention. Organizations like RAINN (Rape, Abuse & Incest National Network) report that an American is sexually assaulted with alarming frequency (RAINN statistics). The National Domestic Violence Hotline highlights that millions experience intimate partner violence annually (National Domestic Violence Hotline data). Child abuse, tracked by entities like Childhelp [31] and government agencies (e.g., U.S. Children's Bureau), continues to affect hundreds of thousands of children each year (Childhelp data). [31] The trauma inflicted by such abuse has profound and long-lasting consequences on individuals' souls, their ability to trust, and their perception of the world.

- **Struggles with Identity and Value:** In an age of shifting cultural narratives and relentless social media comparison, many individuals, particularly young adults, grapple intensely with questions of identity, value, and purpose. More broadly, the pressure to conform to certain images, achieve particular statuses, or find worth in external validation leaves many feeling adrift, insecure, and questioning their intrinsic value.

For a church committed to being "impious Galileans" in the world, these realities of relational fracture, abuse, and identity crises are not peripheral concerns. They are mission-critical areas where the radical love, justice, and healing power of the Gospel are desperately needed. To turn away, or to offer simplistic platitudes, is to fail the very people Christ consistently moved towards.

The Church's Response: Falling Short and Striving Forward

The church, as a divinely ordained institution intended to be a beacon of hope and healing, has a complex record when it comes to addressing these deep societal and personal wounds. There are countless stories of individuals finding solace, support, and restoration within loving church communities. Many churches strive to offer compassionate care, support groups for those navigating divorce or grief, and ministries aimed at upholding the sanctity of relationships and the dignity of every person.

However, candor requires acknowledging areas where the church has fallen short, and at times, even contributed to the pain.

- **Mishandling of Abuse:** High-profile (and countless less public) cases of churches mishandling allegations of abuse—whether by prioritizing institutional reputation over victim care, disbelieving survivors, or lacking proper protocols for prevention and response—have caused immense harm and eroded trust (general knowledge from media investigations and reports by organizations like GRACE). [32]

- **Judgmental or Simplistic Counsel:** Individuals facing divorce, wrestling with their identity, or healing from trauma have sometimes encountered judgment, shame, or overly simplistic theological answers within church settings, rather than the deep empathy, understanding, and long-term support they desperately need.

- **The Allure of Inauthenticity:** In a culture drawn to image and influence, even some church leadership can fall prey to a "cool pastor" syndrome. This can manifest as a focus on attracting a certain demographic—often young, "attractive," and successful—by emphasizing trendy branding, name-dropping connections to celebrities or luxury brands, and creating an exclusive "elite" feel. Such environments, often lacking in genuine financial transparency and sometimes even preaching "bought" or shallow sermons focused on self-improvement rather than deep discipleship, can further alienate those who are broken and seeking authenticity. This focus on building a leader's personal brand rather than fostering a truly safe, godly, and inclusive community is the antithesis of the servant leadership modeled by Christ and the "impious Galileans." It can leave those who don't fit the "brand" feeling more marginalized and their deeper wounds unaddressed.

The "impious Galileans," by contrast, created a radically different social reality. Their communities were not built on exclusivity, brand appeal, or the charisma of a single leader, but on shared vulnerability, mutual care, and a commitment to living out the sacrificial love of Jesus. For the modern church to become a true agent of healing in these fractured areas, it must strive to embody that ancient, yet ever-relevant, Galilean spirit. This involves not only a desire to do good but a rigorous commitment to creating cultures of safety, demonstrating profound empathy, and courageously confronting areas where its own practices may have fallen short of the compassionate heart of its Founder.

Galilean Principles for Healing and Restoration

In stark contrast to societal brokenness and any institutional failings of the church, the way of the "impious Galileans" offers enduring principles for fostering healing and restoration. Their community was not perfect, but its core ethos, derived from the teachings and example of Jesus, provided a radically different environment for those wounded by relational fractures, abuse, and identity struggles. To become a true agent of mending in our modern world, the church must actively cultivate these Galilean principles:

- **Radical Acceptance and Unconditional Belonging:** The early Christian communities were revolutionary in their inclusivity. In a world rigidly stratified by social status, ethnicity, and gender, they offered a community where such distinctions were secondary to a shared identity in Christ. Individuals who were divorced, widowed, orphaned, former outcasts, or simply "othered" by society could find a place of genuine belonging and acceptance. This was not a tolerance that glossed over sin, but a profound welcome into a family that offered grace and a path to wholeness. For those today wrestling with the shame of a broken marriage, the stigma of abuse, or confusion about their identity, a modern Galilean church must be a place where they are first and foremost embraced with the unconditional love of God, assured that their inherent worth is not diminished by their experiences or struggles. This principle of radical acceptance is the starting point for all healing.

- **Unyielding Commitment to Justice and Protection of the Vulnerable:** The "impious Galileans" were known for their extraordinary care for the most vulnerable members of society—the poor, the sick, widows, orphans, and even strangers. This commitment was not mere sentimentality but a deep-seated conviction about God's justice and special concern for those at risk. A modern church embodying this principle will:

  - Take a fierce, unequivocal stand against all forms of abuse, creating and enforcing robust policies for prevention and response.

  - Prioritize the safety and well-being of victims, offering them tangible support, belief, and pathways to justice and healing, rather than protecting abusers or institutional reputation.

  - Advocate for the marginalized and those whose voices are often silenced, reflecting God's heart for justice in practical ways.

This protective, justice-oriented stance is crucial for rebuilding trust with those who have been harmed and for demonstrating that the church is a safe haven, not a place where wounds are ignored or exacerbated. ...This protective, justice-oriented stance is crucial for rebuilding trust with those who have been harmed and for demonstrating that the church is a safe haven, not a place where wounds are ignored or exacerbated.

- **Profound Affirmation of Inherent Worth Rooted in Divine Creation:** In a world that often assigns value based on appearance, achievement, relationships, or societal labels, the Christian message offers a radically different foundation for self-worth: every human being is created in the image of God (*Imago Dei*) (Genesis 1:26-27) and possesses immeasurable, inherent dignity. The "impious Galileans" lived out this truth by valuing each individual. A modern Galilean church must consistently teach, model, and celebrate this truth. For individuals struggling with a diminished sense of self due to past abuse, relational failure, or societal pressures regarding identity, the church should be the primary community where they are unequivocally reminded of their belovedness by God and their intrinsic worth, independent of their circumstances or struggles. This affirmation is foundational for rebuilding a healthy sense of identity.

- **Pathways to Forgiveness, Healing, and (Where Possible and Safe) Reconciliation:** The Gospel is, at its core, a message of reconciliation—first with God, and then, as far as it depends on us, with one another (2 Corinthians 5:18-20). The early Christians practiced processes of accountability and restoration (as seen in Matthew 18). A modern Galilean church recognizes that healing from relational wounds and abuse is a complex journey that often involves:

  - Supporting individuals through processes of grieving and healing from trauma.

  - Teaching and modeling healthy relational dynamics and boundaries.

  - Offering pathways to forgiveness—both for those who have been wronged (as a means of their own freedom, not as an excuse for abusers) and for those who have caused harm and are genuinely repentant.

- Facilitating reconciliation in relationships where it is safe, healthy, and desired by all parties, while also recognizing that some relationships, particularly abusive ones, may necessitate permanent separation for safety and well-being.

This nuanced approach, grounded in both grace and truth, is essential for mending the torn fabric of people's lives.

By actively embodying these principles—radical acceptance, unwavering justice, profound affirmation of worth, and pathways to healing—the church can begin to mirror the restorative community of the early "impious Galileans." It can become a place where the divorced find compassion, not condemnation; where survivors of abuse find safety and advocacy, not skepticism; and where those wrestling with their identity find love, guidance, and a secure foundation in Christ.

Creating a Culture of Safety, Healing, and True Identity in Christ

Embodying the Galilean principles of acceptance, justice, affirmation, and restoration requires more than good intentions; it demands the intentional creation of a church culture where safety is paramount, healing is actively pursued, and individuals are discipled into their true identity in Christ. This stands in stark contrast to any church environment where image, exclusivity, or a leader's personal brand take precedence over the genuine well-being and spiritual health of its people. A truly "impious Galilean" church prioritizes substance over style, and safety over superficial appeal. Here are practical steps for cultivating such a culture:

Implement and Enforce Robust Safety and Protection Policies:

- **Zero Tolerance for Abuse:** Churches must have clear, comprehensive, and publicly accessible policies regarding child protection, abuse prevention (for all ages), and response to allegations. This includes mandatory reporting procedures, background checks for all staff and volunteers working with vulnerable populations, and clear consequences for perpetrators. Criminals need to be reported to the police, not managed through internal control mechanisms.

- **Victim-Centered Approach:** When allegations arise, the immediate priority must be the care and safety of the alleged victim. This means believing them, providing support, and ensuring investigations are handled by independent, qualified professionals, not solely by internal leadership, which can lead to conflicts of interest.

- **Transparency in Process:** While respecting individual privacy, transparency about the existence of safety policies and the church's commitment to upholding them builds trust. This is the opposite of cultures that seek to cover up or minimize abuse to protect institutional reputation.

Provide Trauma-Informed Care and Support:

- **Educate Leaders and Congregants:** Offer training on the nature of trauma and its impact. Understanding how trauma affects individuals helps create a more empathetic and supportive environment.

- **Develop or Partner for Support Groups:** Facilitate or host support groups for individuals healing from specific traumas like abuse, divorce, grief, or addiction. These groups should be led by trained facilitators who can create a safe space for sharing and healing.

- **Mindful Ministry Practices:** Ensure that preaching, teaching, and ministry practices are sensitive to those who may have experienced trauma, avoiding language or approaches that could inadvertently trigger or re-traumatize.

Offer Compassionate and Non-Judgmental Ministry for Relational Brokenness:

- **Divorce Care:** Provide compassionate support for individuals and families navigating the pain of divorce, offering practical help, emotional support, and a non-judgmental community, rather than condemnation or simplistic solutions.

- **Marriage and Family Support:** Proactively invest in resources and ministries that strengthen marriages and families, focusing on healthy communication, conflict resolution, and mutual respect, which can help prevent some forms of relational breakdown.

Disciple People in Their True Identity in Christ:

- **Counteract False Narratives:** Actively teach and preach about the believer's true identity as a beloved, chosen, and adopted child of God, an identity that is secure and not dependent on performance, relationships, societal approval, or worldly measures of success. [33] This directly counters the identity crises fueled by cultural pressures.

- **Emphasize Inherent Worth:** Consistently affirm the inherent worth and dignity of every individual as created in God's image, regardless of their past, their struggles, or how they identify in other spheres.

- **Freedom from Comparison and Performance:** Foster a church culture that liberates people from the trap of comparison and performance-based acceptance. True discipleship focuses on growth in grace and Christ-likeness, not on achieving an artificial standard of spiritual "success" or conforming to an exclusive "brand".

Cultivate Authentic Leadership and Financial Transparency:

- **Servant Leadership as the Model:** Ensure that church leadership models humility, service, and integrity, rather than the self-promoting, image-conscious style of the "cool pastor" phenomenon. Leadership should be about empowering others and building up the community, not a personal platform.

- **Financial Integrity and Openness:** As discussed in Chapter 7, financial transparency is crucial. When a church is open about its finances and how resources are stewarded, it builds trust and demonstrates that its priority is mission and ministry, not the enrichment or branding of an elite few. This integrity is vital for creating a safe environment where people feel their contributions are honored.

By diligently pursuing these practical steps, a church moves beyond merely *talking* about being a healing community and actively *becomes* one. It creates a culture where the "torn fabric" of people's lives can be gently mended, where safety allows for vulnerability, where compassionate care facilitates healing, and where individuals are empowered to embrace their true, God-given identity. This is the painstaking, often unseen, but deeply transformative work of a modern "impious Galilean" community.

Conclusion: The Impious Galilean Church – A Restorer of Breaches, A Shelter for the Broken

The landscape of modern life, as we have seen, is littered with the casualties of fractured relationships, the deep scars of abuse, and the pervasive ache of uncertain identities. These are not peripheral issues but profound wounds that tear at the very fabric of individual lives and societal well-being. For the church to embody the spirit of the "impious Galileans" in such a world, it must be unequivocally committed to being a community that actively mends, protects, and restores.

We've acknowledged the church's own journey in this area, with moments of both faithful care and regrettable failure. The path forward, however, is not one of defensive denial or superficial fixes, but a humble and courageous embrace of the Galilean principles of radical acceptance, unwavering justice for the oppressed, profound affirmation of every individual's inherent worth in Christ, and a commitment to walking with people through the difficult pathways of healing and, where possible and safe, reconciliation. This stands in direct opposition to any form of leadership or church culture that prioritizes image, exclusivity, or self-aggrandizement over the genuine care and safety of its people.

Creating a culture of true safety—where abuse is confronted and prevented, where victims are believed and supported, and where confidentiality and professionalism are paramount—is non-negotiable. It is the bedrock upon which ministries of healing for the divorced, for survivors of abuse, and for those wrestling with their identity can be built. When the church intentionally fosters such an environment, it ceases to be just another institution; it becomes what Isaiah prophesied Christ's people would be: "a repairer of the breach, a restorer of streets to live in" (Isaiah 58:12, paraphrased).

The "impious Galileans" were distinct because they lived out a love that was both fiercely protective of the vulnerable and tenderly restorative to the broken. For the contemporary church to reclaim this legacy, it must be willing to engage with the messy, painful realities of people's lives, offering not platitudes, but the steadfast, healing presence of Christ. In doing so, it becomes a true shelter for those battered by life's storms, a sanctuary where the torn fabric of lives and relationships can be patiently and lovingly mended, and where every individual can discover their unshakable value as a beloved child of God. This is the calling of a truly counter-cultural, fiercely compassionate, and undeniably relevant Galilean church.

PART 5

THE FIERCE FUTURE – A COUNTER-CULTURAL MOVEMENT ONCE MORE

CHAPTER 18

THE TRANSFORMATIVE POWER OF A COUNTER-CULTURAL MOVEMENT: BECOMING "HATED FOR THE RIGHT REASON"

The vision of the church reclaiming its "impious Galilean" identity culminates in a profound transformation: becoming "hated for the right reason". This concept, far from advocating for animosity, suggests that when the church authentically embodies the radical counter-culturalism of early Christianity—its self-sacrificial love, boundless generosity, unwavering commitment to justice, and uncompromising adherence to Christ's teachings—it will inevitably challenge prevailing societal norms and power structures. Such a challenge, while often met with resistance, is a hallmark of a church truly living out its calling.

For too long, the modern church has feared being disliked, and in its pursuit of cultural relevance and acceptance, it has often muted its prophetic voice and blunted its distinctive edge. The result is a faith that is too often perceived as hypocritical, politically co-opted, or simply irrelevant—hated, if at all, for all the wrong reasons. [34] The "impious Galileans" faced hatred not because they were weak or compromised, but because they were strong and uncompromising in their love and their allegiance to a different King and Kingdom. Julian the Apostate did not despise them for being ineffectual; he was threatened by their effectiveness, their communal solidarity, and a charity so potent he tried, and failed, to replicate it.

To be hated for the right reason means our love for the poor and marginalized is so extravagant it exposes the greed and indifference of the world. It means our commitment to truth and integrity is so unyielding it rebukes the duplicity and cynicism of the age. It means our vision of community is so inclusive and restorative it stands as a judgment against the world's divisions and hierarchies. It means our ultimate hope is so firmly fixed on the coming Kingdom of God that we are liberated from the fear and idolatry of earthly power.

This is the fierce future of a counter-cultural movement. It is not a future where the church seeks conflict, but one where it refuses to shrink from the necessary friction that arises when the light of the Gospel confronts the darkness. It is a future where our reputation is forged not by our cultural savvy, but by our Christ-like character. When the world looks at us and sees a people whose love is undeniable, whose joy is unquenchable, and whose hope is unshakable, some will be drawn to the light, and others, inevitably, will resent it. To be hated for that reason is not a sign of failure, but a profound mark of faithfulness.

CHAPTER 19

THE END OF AN ERA: THE DEATH OF JULIAN AND THE TRIUMPH OF CHRISTIANITY

The Final Campaign and the Philosopher's Death

The Persian expedition, which Julian envisioned as the crowning achievement of his reign, a campaign to rival Alexander's, became his undoing. In the scorching summer of 363 AD, the Roman army was lured deep into Sassanian territory. While Julian had achieved early victories, the campaign strategy faltered. Harassed by a mobile enemy and facing dwindling supplies after a disastrous decision to burn his own fleet of supply ships, the emperor found his legions in a perilous retreat.

On June 26th, during a chaotic rearguard skirmish, Julian, ever the frontline commander, characteristically plunged into the fray. In his haste, he had neglected to don his cuirass. A Persian spear, thrown from an unknown hand, struck him in the side, lodging deep in his liver.

Carried back to his tent, the philosopher-emperor met his end with a composure that impressed even his Christian detractors. The historian Ammianus Marcellinus, an eyewitness on the campaign, provides a detailed account. Surrounded by his distraught generals and his philosopher friends, Maximus and Priscus, Julian delivered a final oration. He expressed contentment with his fate, grateful to the "eternal substance of the heavens" for a clean death on the battlefield rather than a slow decay from illness or the blade of a conspirator. He spoke of the soul, of his stewardship of the empire, and faced his mortality not as a defeated emperor, but as a philosopher serenely accepting the course of nature.

"Thou Hast Conquered, O Galilean"

The historical record of Julian's last words is split by the ideological chasm of the age. The pagan and secular accounts, like that of Ammianus, paint a picture of Stoic resignation.

However, a far more dramatic and enduring version emerged from Christian chroniclers. Theodoret, Bishop of Cyrrhus, [3] writing several decades later, claimed that as the spear struck, Julian scooped blood from his wound, flung it towards the sky, and uttered the defiant cry: "Νενίκηκας, Γαλιλαῖε" (Nenikēkas, Galilaîe) — "Thou hast conquered, O Galilean."

While virtually no modern historian believes Julian spoke these words—they are widely considered a masterful piece of theological propaganda—their invention and subsequent popularity reveal a more profound truth. The phrase perfectly encapsulated the sentiment of the triumphant Church. Julian's project to revive Hellenic paganism was so deeply tied to his own person that it could not survive him. Whether he admitted it or not, his death on the plains of Mesopotamia sealed the victory of the faith he had so passionately rejected.

The Victory of the Galileans

The "victory of the Galileans" was immediate and absolute. With the emperor dead and the army stranded deep in enemy territory, the commanders hastily elected a successor. Their choice was Jovian, a senior officer of the imperial guard and, crucially, a devout Nicene Christian.

Jovian's brief, eight-month reign was marked by two momentous decisions. First, to save the starving army, he negotiated a humiliating peace with the Sassanian King, Shapur II. Rome surrendered five provinces east of the Tigris and abandoned its key fortresses in the region, a devastating blow to its eastern frontier that erased decades of military gains.

Second, and of more lasting significance, Jovian systematically dismantled Julian's religious reforms. He immediately restored the Labarum—the military standard bearing the Christian Chi-Rho (☧) that Constantine had made famous—to its place of honor. He ended state funding for pagan sacrifices and restored the privileges, stipends, and properties to the Christian clergy that Julian had rescinded.

The Foundations of the Galilean Victory

Yet, the triumph of Christianity was not merely the result of an opportune death and a swift political reversal. Its foundations were deeper, built upon a revolutionary social structure that paganism could not match. Julian himself, in a letter to a pagan high priest, identified the Christians' greatest weapon with frustrated admiration: their virtue.

He wrote that the "impiety of the Galileans" was fueled by their "philanthropy towards strangers... their care in burying the dead, and their feigned holiness of life." This was a stunning admission. The Christian emphasis on **kindness, generosity, and love (agape)** was not just a theological concept; it was a strategic advantage. As scholars like Rodney Stark have argued, Christianity's growth was explosive because it functioned as a "society within a society," an engine of mutual support that proved its worth most vividly in times of crisis. During the devastating plagues that ravaged the empire, pagan priests and physicians fled the cities; Christians, by contrast, stayed to nurse both their own and their pagan neighbors, demonstrating a high-risk, high-commitment love that was impossible to ignore. Their survival rates were higher, and their communities became islands of stability and hope in a sea of terror.

The death of Julian the Apostate was the death knell for institutional paganism. His great "Apostasy" had proven to be a brilliant but fragile intellectual movement, dependent on the force of one man's will. With that man gone, the tide of history—a tide powered by charity, community, and a transformative message of love—resumed its inexorable course. The Galilean had, in fact, conquered.

The Crucible's Aftermath: A Church Forged for Service

The trial under Julian, though brief, acted as a crucible for the Church. His opposition, particularly his attempt to co-opt their methods of charity, forced Christians to clarify and deepen their own motivations. His pressure did not break them; it forged them. When the threat passed, the Church did not simply return to the status quo. It emerged with a renewed resolve and a more focused understanding of its social mission.

This forged conviction blossomed into unprecedented social action in the decades that followed. It was in this very period, in the direct aftermath of Julian's reign, that the Church began to institutionalize its compassion on a scale never before seen. The most famous example is the 'Basiliad,' founded by St. Basil the Great in Caesarea just a few years after Julian's death. This was not merely a hostel or a soup kitchen; it was a massive, integrated complex—a "new city" dedicated to mercy. It included a hospital with professional medical staff, a hospice for the terminally ill, a leprosarium for those with leprosy, an orphanage, and a shelter for the homeless.

The Basiliad was a direct, tangible answer to Julian's failed pagan version. It demonstrated that Christian charity was not an artificial policy but the natural outflow of a faith centered on a God who became poor for our sake. This model of comprehensive, institutional care, born from the conviction of the post-Julian church, became a blueprint. It inspired the creation of similar institutions across the empire, laying the groundwork for the entire Western tradition of public hospitals and organized social welfare. The persecution had forced the Church to prove its faith through works, and the result was the creation of a social safety net that would forever change the landscape of compassion and human flourishing.

CHAPTER 20

LIVING AS MODERN-DAY IMPIOUS GALILEANS: A LOVE THAT ECHOES ETERNITY

We stand at the culmination of a journey, a re-examination of a faith that once turned the world upside down, embodied by those derisively yet accurately termed "impious Galileans". We have explored their historical distinctiveness, contrasted it with the challenges and shortcomings of the contemporary church, and charted pathways toward reclaiming their fierce, counter-cultural spirit. Now, the question lands squarely before us: How then shall we live? What does it mean, in the grit and grace of our 21st-century lives, to embody this ancient yet ever-relevant way of being Christian?

The Wellspring of Our Fierceness: His Love First

The starting point, the unshakable foundation for any attempt to live as a modern-day "impious Galilean," is not our effort, our strategy, or our moral fortitude, but the overwhelming, antecedent love of God. The Apostle John encapsulates it perfectly: "We love because He first loved us" (1 John 4:19). Our capacity for radical generosity, for courageous witness, for sacrificial service, and for counter-cultural kindness flows directly from the wellspring of God's prior love demonstrated most profoundly in Jesus Christ. It is His amazing sacrificial life, freely given, that secured our forgiveness, ushered us into an intimate relationship with God the Father, and sealed for us the unbreakable promise of heaven. Without this experiential grounding in His initiating love and unmerited grace, any attempt to live a fiercely compassionate life will eventually devolve into legalism, burnout, or self-righteousness. But when our hearts are truly captivated by the depth of His love for us—while we were yet sinners—we are liberated and compelled to love in return.

Worthy is the Lamb: Living in Response to His Sacrifice

Flowing from this understanding of God's love is the profound truth that the Lamb that was slain is worthy to receive the reward of His suffering. This is perhaps the most powerful motivational force for a life of radical mission. It is perfectly captured in the historic account of the first Moravian missionaries in the 18th century. When hearing of an island in the West Indies where enslaved Africans were unable to hear the Gospel, two young men, Leonard Dober [5] and David Nitschmann, [35] volunteered to go. The story is told that they were willing to sell themselves into slavery to reach these souls, and as the ship pulled away from the shore, they cried out a final, defining message to the community they were leaving behind: **"May the Lamb that was slain receive the reward of His suffering!"**

This was not mere slogan; it was a worldview. It reframed their entire sacrifice. Their lives, their freedom, their very bodies were not a loss, but a small offering to ensure that the Lamb who suffered so much would receive the full reward He was due—the worship and redemption of people from every tribe, tongue, and nation. This perspective shifts our motivation from duty to devotion, from obligation to overflow. We live differently not to earn His favor, but because His favor has already so lavishly been poured out upon us. This desire to honor His sacrifice becomes a powerful internal driver for the kind of whole-life discipleship that character-ized the early Galileans.

The Everyday Marks of an Impious Galilean: Love in Action

This devoted, responsive love is not meant to remain an ab-stract internal sentiment; it must take on flesh and blood in the everyday realities of our lives. What does this look like practically?

- **Inner Postures Flowing Outward:** It begins in the heart, cultivating a spirit that is quick to forgive and slow to hold grudges, recognizing the immense forgiveness we our-selves have received. It means embracing repentance not as a one-time act but as a lifestyle of turning towards God. It calls us to live honestly and with integrity in all our dealings, and to exude a genuine kindness that reflects the kindness of God.

- **Counter-Cultural Kindness and Consideration:** In a world often marked by entitlement and self-absorption— the "Ken and Karen" culture of complaints and demands— the (impious Galilean) stands out. This looks like inten-tionally tipping well and with a generous spirit, especially on Sundays after church but consistently throughout the week, recognizing the service of others. It's in the small, often unnoticed acts, like returning the shopping cart to its proper place instead of leaving it for someone else to deal with. These simple actions communicate a profound respect and consideration for others.

- **Bearing Burdens and Sharing Pain:** The Galilean spirit compels us to move towards those who are suffering. This means a willingness to take in others' weight and pain, to listen with empathy, and to offer practical sup-port. It means taking the time to visit a hospital or a nurs-ing home, to sit with a hurting friend who is grieving or struggling, and to simply be present in their sorrow.

- **Other-Centered Living:** Ultimately, all these actions are summed up in a life that intentionally makes itself about the "other". Because of Jesus' amazing sacrificial life that purchased our forgiveness and relationship with God, we are freed from the bondage of self-centeredness to live for something—and Someone—greater.

Love as the Indispensable Quality: Avoiding the "Clanging Cymbal"

The Apostle Paul's profound meditation on love in 1 Corinthians 13 serves as both an inspiration and a sober warning. We can possess all manner of spiritual gifts, engage in heroic acts of service, and even sacrifice our bodies, but if we "have not love," we are nothing more than a "noisy gong or a clanging cymbal". All the characteristics of the "impious Galilean"—their radical generosity, their zealous evangelism, their disciplined community, their commitment to justice—must be animated and infused by genuine, Christ-like love. Without it, our fierceness can become harshness, our truth can become weaponized, and our service can become self-serving. Love is the indispensable quality that makes our witness authentic and compelling.

The Bride, The Return, and The Present Imperative: Don't Wait, Be Now!

The Church is described as the Bride of Christ, eagerly awaiting and preparing for His return. This glorious eschatological hope should not, however, lead to a passive disengagement from the world's present needs and Christ's present commands. Indeed, it should do the opposite. Knowing that our King is returning should fuel an urgent, joyful, and proactive embodiment of the "impious Galilean" spirit today. We don't wait for a future heavenly reality to begin living out Kingdom values; we are called to incarnate those values now, in this time, in this place. The anticipation of His return is not a call to huddle in fear or retreat in judgment, but to go forth in love and power, working to "bring all to know Him" by demonstrating the goodness and beauty of His reign in our lives and communities.

Final Exhortation: Go and Be Impious Galileans

The journey is over, but the path has just begun. The path of the "impious Galilean" is not a historical curiosity; it is a summons to your soul, a call to a radical, all-of-life Christianity that refuses to be tamed, compartmentalized, or silenced. It is a clarion call to be so utterly and thoroughly saturated with the love and character of Jesus Christ that our very way of being becomes a seismic challenge to the status quo. It is a charge to live a life that offers tangible hope to the despairing soul, brings restorative healing to the broken-hearted, and relentlessly points all people toward the beautiful, world-altering, transformative power of the Gospel.

This is a call as a Body to live with such unassailable integrity that it exposes deceit, such profound compassion that it shames indifference, and such quiet courage that it defies fear. It is a call for the church to live in a way that the world, even if it misunderstands, resents, or dislikes us for our "impiety" towards its idols of power, wealth, and self, cannot logically deny the goodness and power of the God we serve. Let them be perplexed by our joy in suffering, baffled by our generosity, and undone by our love. For love is the "indispensable quality"; it is the fire that makes our sacrifice burn brightly and the melody that turns our noisy gongs into a symphony of grace, making our witness authentic and compelling.

Finally, let the glorious, certain hope of Christ's return not be a sedative that leads to passive disengagement, but the very fuel for our urgency. It should ignite a joyful, relentless, and immediate embodiment of the "impious Galilean" spirit today. We are not called to simply wait for a future reality to live out Kingdom values; we are commanded and empowered to incarnate those values now, in our churches, in our homes, in our workplaces, and in our communities. The Bride does not wait idly; she makes herself ready.

Therefore, go. Embrace this ancient, yet desperately needed, way. Go and love fiercely, serve sacrificially, forgive freely, and live honestly. Go and be the hands that restore, the feet that run to the outcast, and the heart that breaks for what breaks God's own. Go and become modern-day "impious Galileans"—community of people whose lives make the good news of Jesus Christ utterly, undeniably, and irresistibly true. Let us not wait for a more convenient season, but be His presence in the world now, until He comes again.

SOJOURN WITH US: AN INVITATION TO JOIN THE MOVEMENT

We have journeyed through history, confronted the challenges of our present moment, and cast a vision for a fierce, counter-cultural future. We have reclaimed the moniker of "Impious Galilean" not as an insult, but as a standard—a call to embody a faith so authentic, so compassionate, and so transformative that it changes the world around it. The final question posed in these pages was, "How then shall we live?"

The path forward is twofold. It involves the courageous transformation of our churches and organizations as institutions, and it requires the empowerment of every believer to become a minister in their unique, God-given vocation. Translating these principles from the page into your specific context is the next vital step. You are not alone in this endeavor.

The Galilean Group was formed to come alongside you. We exist to help you move from inspiration to implementation.

For Your Church or Organization

For pastors, deacons, board members, and ministry leaders, we offer partnership in reforging your community into a hub of missional power. We can help you:

- **Inspire Your Community:** Ignite vision and passion through powerful teaching and preaching. We offer conference keynotes, Sunday morning preaching, and a four-part, half-day journey with the author to challenge and encourage your entire group.

- **Sharpen Your Strategy:** Move from vision to a concrete plan with our hands-on consulting and facilitation. Through **Two-Day Executive Offsites**, we help you diagnose your "internal gravitation" and build a strategic roadmap toward financial reformation and radical generosity. With ongoing **Fractional Leadership**, we embed one of our experienced leaders into your team to provide the strategic counsel and operational support needed to navigate lasting change.

For You and Your Vocation

The spirit of the Impious Galilean is not confined to church walls. It is a charge for every business leader, non-profit director, and follower of Christ in the marketplace to be a force for redemptive change. We provide tailored consulting to help you:

- Integrate a Galilean ethos of integrity and audacious generosity into your business model.

- Cultivate a culture of purpose that transforms your workplace and serves the common good.

- Align your professional life with a counter-cultural mission that echoes eternity.

This is more than a new set of programs; it is a call to join a groundswell. It is an invitation to build a new kind of church—or rather, to reclaim the oldest and most potent kind—a church that is, once again, hated for all the right reasons.

The path of the Impious Galilean is not easy, but it is the path to a fierce, world-transforming movement.

To begin the conversation, visit us at **www.GalileanGroup.com** or email us at **info@GalileanGroup.com**.

ACKNOWLEDGMENTS

This journey begins and ends with family. To my Mom and Dad, as you celebrate over 50 years of ministry and marriage, you have set an unbelievable example. You never charged a dime for ministry, often to your own hurt, and were so committed to your work in Africa that you would frequently return with less than you had when you left. I grew up watching you stay up all night with failing pastors and loving your friends and neighbors so well. For your commitment to Jesus, your unrelenting prayers, and your love and support in the good and trying times, thank you. I am proud of you both.

To my sister Amy, my brother-in-law Jesse, and my niece and nephews, Bella, Jet, and Cash, I love you all. Thank you for letting me be your brother and uncle. To Gerald and Dee (Ooma and GG), thank you for showing us unrelenting love and support when we had nowhere else to turn; you have always been there for us. We love you both! To my mother-in-law, Tammy and my father-in-law Tony for believing in us. To Grandpa David and Grandma Sharon, thank you for your love.

GLOSSARY

80/20 Rule: A principle, also known as the Pareto principle, which in a church context often describes the reality where 80% of the ministry work is done by 20% of the people. This book advocates for a model that overcomes this imbalance.

Abba: An Aramaic term of endearment for "father," akin to "daddy" or "papa." In the New Testament, it signifies a deeply intimate and personal relationship with God as Father, made possible for believers through the Holy Spirit.

Apologetics: The practice of offering a reasoned defense and justification of the Christian faith. It involves engaging with questions, objections, and alternative worldviews to articulate the truth and coherence of Christian beliefs.

Apostle (as a five-fold ministry gift): One of the leadership gifts mentioned in Ephesians 4:11, given to the church for equipping believers. While the original twelve apostles held a unique foundational role, the ongoing apostolic function or gifting often involves pioneering new missional works, laying spiritual foundations in churches, providing spiritual parenting and oversight to leaders, ensuring doctrinal integrity, and offering strategic wisdom for the broader body of Christ.

Benevolence: Acts of kindness, charity, and practical assistance offered to those in need, particularly the poor and marginalized. In the context of the book, it refers to the church's direct aid and compassionate care, reflecting God's love and contrasting with mere institutional maintenance.

CarePortal: [27] A technology platform and ministry initiative that connects local child welfare workers with nearby churches and community members who can respond to the real-time, tangible needs of vulnerable children and families in crisis.

Celsus: A 2nd-century Greek philosopher and prominent critic of early Christianity. His writings, though largely known through Origen's refutation ("Contra Celsum"), provide valuable (though hostile) external perspectives on early Christian beliefs and practices, such as the active evangelism by ordinary believers.

Charity: While often used interchangeably with benevolence, in the context of this book, "charity" generally refers to acts of giving, aid, and love extended to those in need, often motivated by compassion and religious conviction. The term is particularly used when discussing the early Christians' notable care for both their own and for outsiders, a practice that distinguished them in the Roman world. The book also explores how the term "charity" in modern church budgets can sometimes be ambiguously defined, potentially obscuring the actual extent of direct aid to the poor.

City Movements: Collaborative efforts, often involving multiple churches, Christian organizations, and community leaders, aimed at the holistic transformation (spiritual, social, cultural, economic) of a specific city or urban area. These movements typically emphasize a "go congregation" ethos, empowering believers to live out their faith redemptively in all spheres of society for the common good and the *shalom* of their city.

Community First! Village: An innovative master-planned community in Austin, Texas, developed by Mobile Loaves & Fishes. It provides affordable, permanent housing and a supportive community for men and women coming out of chronic homelessness, offering services and fostering a sense of belonging. [28]

Corpus permixtum: A Latin term meaning "mixed body." In theological discussions of the church, it refers to the understanding that the visible church on earth is composed of both genuine believers and those who may not be truly regenerate, existing together until the final judgment. The book references this in the context of the church's institutionalization in the 4th century.

Culture Making (Andy Crouch concept): A framework, prominently articulated by author Andy Crouch, that encourages Christians to move beyond merely consuming, copying, or condemning culture, and instead to become active "cultivators" and "creators." This involves tending and nourishing what is best in human culture and daring to create new things that make the world more welcoming, thrilling, and beautiful, reflecting God's creativity and redemptive purposes. [18]

Full Employment Policy (John Jackson concept): A term used to describe a church culture that stands in direct contrast to the 80/20 rule. It is a vision for the Body of Christ where every member is activated and empowered for ministry according to their unique, God-given gifts and calling.

Go Congregation / Come Congregation: A distinction in church missiology. A "Come Congregation" primarily focuses on attracting people to its building and internal programs. A "Go Congregation," a concept emphasized by leaders like Roger Valci, focuses on equipping and sending its members out into the community to be the church and minister where they live, work, and play, reflecting an outward, missional posture.

Imago Dei: A Latin theological term meaning "Image of God." It refers to the biblical concept that human beings are created in God's likeness, possessing inherent dignity, value, and certain capacities that reflect, albeit imperfectly, those of their Creator.

Impious Galileans: The derogatory term used by the Roman Emperor Julian the Apostate to describe early Christians, particularly those from Galilee. The book re-appropriates this label as a badge of honor, symbolizing a commitment to radical, counter-cultural faith, sacrificial love, and transformative community engagement that challenges prevailing societal norms.

Up, In, Out (Randy Frazee [14] concept): A framework for understanding and assessing balanced, holistic discipleship. It emphasizes three vital relationships: with God (Up), with fellow believers in authentic community (In), and with the world through mission and service (Out).

ABOUT THE AUTHOR

Mike Brock is a second-generation pastor whose formative years in a vibrant ministry household instilled in him a deep and enduring love for the Church. This passion has fueled more than two decades of leadership and service, shaping his vision to see the Church flourish in unity, maturity, and lasting impact.

Guided by Ephesians 4:13—"until we all reach unity in the faith and in the knowledge of the Son of God and become mature, attaining to the whole measure of the fullness of Christ"—Mike is deeply committed to the Church's mission of equipping believers, cultivating spiritual maturity, and embodying the transformative presence of Christ in the world. This scripture serves as both an anchor and a call to action in his ministry, driving his efforts to strengthen and renew the Church's role in contemporary society.

For nearly 20 years, Mike has served as a pastor and organizational leader, focusing on systemic transformation and organizational health across diverse sectors, including non-profit, education, government, business, and—most importantly—faith-based communities. As Managing Partner of The Galilean Group, he leads a team that partners with churches and Christian nonprofits to enhance leadership capacity, improve organizational effectiveness, and foster long-term vitality. Their work includes executive off-sites, leadership coaching, team development, and strategic planning—each initiative aimed at building strong, mission-driven organizations.

Mike's expertise spans executive leadership, strategic planning, budget and operational oversight, team building, and conflict resolution. He has also helped churches develop small group curricula and create meaningful partnerships with local nonprofits, mobilizing congregations to engage in tangible acts of service—an echo of the early Church's powerful witness in the world.

He holds a Master of Arts in Theology (Cross-Cultural Studies) from Regent University and speaks nationally to church leaders, executive teams, and organizations seeking to align purpose, health, and impact.

Mike is passionate about equipping churches to thrive—believing that a healthy, unified, and mission-focused Church is essential to building resilient communities and advancing the Gospel in meaningful, lasting ways.

Originally raised in Hawaii during his formative years, Mike spent 16 years in the Bay Area before returning to Honolulu, where he lives with his wife, Ashley, and their three children—Crew, Olive, and Pippa. His family remains his greatest joy and daily motivation in his ongoing commitment to serve and strengthen the Church.

BIBLIOGRAPHY

1. **Palmer, Donovan**. Referenced in the foreword of the book. He is also the CEO of Mission Aviation Fellowship International. Website: *https://maf-uk.org/* (Referenced on page 8)

2. **Julian**. *Against the Galilaeans*. Translated by Wilmer Cave Wright. *In The Works of the Emperor Julian, Vol. 3.* Loeb Classical Library 157. Cambridge, MA: Harvard University Press, 1923. (Referenced on pages 18 & 19)

3. **Theodoret, Bishop of Cyrrhus**. He was a 5th-century Christian bishop, historian, and theologian. He played a key role in the Christological debates of the time and his writings are a major source of information on early church history. (Referenced on pages 19 & 160)

4. **Basilius of Caesarea**. He was a 4th-century bishop and theologian, also known as St. Basil the Great. He is recognized as a key figure in the development of communal monasticism and a defender of Nicene orthodoxy. (Referenced on pages 23 & 41)

5. **Dober, Johann Leonhard**. (Referenced on pages 24 & 166)

6. **Empty tomb, inc.**. "Home Page." Accessed May 29, 2024. *https://emptytomb.org/* (Referenced on pages 33, 55 & 61)

7. **Greer, Peter**. *The Spiritual Danger of Doing Good*. Grand Rapids: Baker Books, 2013. Resources from HOPE International. *https://www.hopeinternational.org/resources/tag/peter+greer* (Referenced on page 33)

8. **Christianity Today's Church Law & Tax Group**. (Referenced on page 33)

9. **Lifeway Research**. "Enlightening Churches With Research & Insights." Accessed August 21, 2024. *https://research.lifeway.com/* (Referenced on page 35)

10. **Bonhoeffer, Dietrich**. *Life Together: The Classic Exploration of Christian Community*. Translated by John W. Doberstein. New York: Harper & Row, 1954. (Referenced on page 43)

11. **Barna Group**. "About Us." Accessed October 18, 2024. *https://www.barna.com/about/* (Referenced on page 49)

12. **Baucham, Voddie**. *Fault Lines: The Social Justice Movement and Evangelicalism's Looming Catastrophe*. Washington, DC: Salem Books, 2023. (Referenced on page 52)

13. **Crosby, Robert**. "Rod and Reel." *Christianity Today*, February 2012. *https://www.christianitytoday.com/2012/02/rodreelnet/* (Referenced on page 79)

14. **Frazee, Randy**. *The Connecting Church: Beyond Small Groups to Authentic Community*. Grand Rapids: Zondervan, 2001. Author and Teacher. *https://www.randyfrazee.com/* (Referenced on pages 86 & 176)

15. **Jackson, John**. *God-Size Your Church*. El Dorado Hills, CA: J. Jackson, 2023. (Referenced on page 101)

16. **Jackson, John**. *Finding Your Place in God's Plan*. Roseville, CA: William Jessup University, 2024. (Referenced on page 102)

17. **Keller, Timothy**. *Every Good Endeavor: Connecting Your Work to God's Work*. New York: Dutton, 2024. (Referenced on page 102)

18. **Crouch, Andy**. *The Tech-Wise Family: Everyday Steps for Putting Technology in Its Proper Place*. Grand Rapids: Baker Books, 2024. (Referenced on pages 105 & 176)

19. **Faith and Work Movement**. "Home." Accessed November 12, 2024. *https://www.faithandworkmovement.org/* (Referenced on page 105)

20. **Faith Driven Movement**. "About." Accessed May 18, 2025. *https://faithdrivenmovements.org/about/*. (Referenced on page 106)

21. **Made to Flourish**. "Faith, Work and Economic Wisdom." Accessed February 12, 2025. *https://www.MadeToFlourish.org/* (Referenced on page 107)

22. **Bradford, Jeff**. *Unleashing the Church: Getting People Out of the Fortress and into the Flow*. San Francisco: Jossey-Bass, 2023. (Referenced on page 109)

23. **Springtide Research Institute**."Terms Of Use." Accessed January 11, 2024. *https://springtideresearch.org/terms-of-use* (Referenced on pages 120, 121 & 122)

24. **Hope for Justice**. "Bringing freedom from human trafficking." Accessed July 28, 2025. *https://hopeforjustice.org/en-us/* (Referenced on pages 127 & 130)

25. **Mobilize Love**. "About Us." Accessed June 25, 2024. *https://www.MobilizeLove.org/about* (Referenced on pages 127 & 130)

26. **Project WeHOPE**. "Mobile Homeless Services" Accessed September 5, 2025. *https://wehope.org/mobilehomelessservices* (Referenced on pages 127 & 130)

27. **CarePortal**. "Home." Accessed April 24, 2024. *https://www.careportal.org/* (Referenced on pages 127, 128, 130 & 174)

28. **Community First! Village**. "Community First! Village." Accessed September 20, 2024. *https://mlf.org/community-first/* (Referenced on pages 127, 130 & 175)

29. **Willard, Dallas**. The book mentions his work on "soul keeping" and spiritual formation. Website: *https://dwillard.org/resources/books* (Referenced on page 132)

30. **Ortberg, John**. *Soul Keeping: Caring for the Most Important Part of You*. Grand Rapids: Zondervan, 2024. (Referenced on page 133)

31. **Childhelp**. "Childhelp National Child Abuse Hotline." Accessed March 15, 2025. *https://www.childhelphotline.org/* (Referenced on page 144)

32. **G.R.A.C.E. (Godly Response to Abuse in the Christian Environment)**. "GRACE." Accessed January 10, 2024. *https://www.netgrace.org/* (Referenced on page 145)

33. **Brooks, Arthur C.**. *From Strength to Strength: Finding Success, Happiness, and Deep Purpose in the Second Half of Life*. New York: Portfolio/Penguin, 2024. (Referenced on page 151)

34. **Amis, Kingsley.** *Lucky Jim*. London: Victor Gollancz, 1954. (Referenced on page 157)

35. **Nitschmann, David**. (Referenced on page 166)

SMALL GROUP CURRICULUM (4-WEEK CYCLE)

Theme: Living as Modern-Day Impious Galileans

Structure: Based on the 4-week rotational model proposed in Chapter 12. Each week includes a brief reading, discussion questions, and a clear action step.

Week 1: Outward-Focused Engagement (The Open House)

- **Prep Reading:** Chapter 9: "Revitalizing Evangelism and Community Engagement."
- **Goal:** To break out of our holy huddles and build genuine relationships with people outside the church.
- **Discussion Questions:**

1. Read the "country club vs. Trader Joe's" analogy. Which one does our group, and our church, feel more like right now? Be honest.

_____

_____

_____

_____

_____

2. The book says the early believers "gossiped the Gospel". What did that look like for them, and what keeps us from sharing our faith as naturally?

_____

_____

_____

_____

_____

3. Who are the specific people in our lives (neighbors, coworkers, school friends) that God has placed on our hearts? Let's make a list.

_____

_____

_____

_____

_____

- **Action Step:**

  - **Plan the "Open House":** As a group, plan a low-pressure social event for the next cycle's "Week 1." This isn't a bait-and-switch Bible study. It's a block party, a BBQ, a game night, or dessert at someone's home. The sole purpose is to build relationships and show Christ's love through hospitality.

  - **This Week's Micro-Action:** Each person commits to inviting *one* person from their list to coffee, lunch, or a walk this week, simply to listen and get to know them better.

Week 2: Rooted in Scripture (Theological Grounding)

- **Prep Reading:** Chapter 3: "Core Characteristics."
- **Goal:** To understand the *theological motivations* that fueled the Galileans' radical lives.
- **Discussion Questions:**

1. Read Matthew 25:40 and James 1:27. The book states the early church's charity had "supernatural value" because serving the "least of these" was serving Christ directly. How does this change our view of generosity from a "budget item" to an act of worship?

_____

_____

_____

_____

_____

2. The book contrasts Julian's "artificial" charity with the Christians' generosity, which flowed from conviction. What convictions about God and money do we need to change in our own hearts?

_____

_____

_____

_____

_____

3. Read about the spiritual disciplines of the early church (prayer, fasting, scripture memory). Why do we often neglect these practices, and how did these *internal* disciplines fuel their *external* impact?

_____

_____

_____

_____

_____

- **Action Step:**
  - **Commit to One Discipline:** As a group, choose one spiritual discipline to practice for the rest of the month (e.g., praying the Lord's Prayer daily, fasting one meal a week, memorizing a key passage like Philippians 2:3-4). Share your experiences next time you meet.

Week 3: Hands-On Community Service (Tangible Love)

- **Prep Reading:** Chapter 14: "The Silent Exodus."
- **Goal:** To move from talking about love to demonstrating it through tangible acts of service.
- **Discussion Questions:**

1. The book lists reasons young people leave the church, including perceived hypocrisy and irrelevance. How does actively serving our community directly combat these perceptions?

_____

_____

_____

_____

_____

2. Read the examples of organizations like Project WeHOPE or Mobilize Love. What are the most pressing, tangible needs in *our* local community (e.g., at a local school, a nursing home, a shelter)?

_____

_____

_____

_____

_____

3. Julian the Apostate was frustrated that Christians cared for *everyone*, not just their own. Who are the "strangers" or marginalized people in our community that we are called to serve?

_____

_____

_____

_____

_____

4. If you can't find somewhere to serve, email us and we will find an opportunity in your community. Email: info@GalileanGroup.com

- **Action Step:**

  - **Serve Together:** This week, instead of just meeting for discussion, the group serves together for 2-3 hours. Volunteer at a local food bank, clean up a park, visit a nursing home, or serve at a ministry your church partners with. This is your meeting. Afterward, spend 15 minutes sharing how the experience impacted you.

Week 4: Communal Accountability (Authentic "Siblingship")

- **Prep Reading:** Chapter 15: "An Epidemic of Despair."

- **Goal:** To create a safe space for the mutual care, confession, and encouragement that sustains a life on mission.

- **Discussion Questions:**

1. The book talks about the church being a "sanctuary for the hurting". On a scale of 1-10, how "safe" does our group feel for sharing real struggles without fear of gossip or judgment?.

   _____

   _____

   _____

   _____

   _____

2. Read Matthew 18:15-17. This passage is about restorative discipline. What does it look like to "bear one another's burdens" (Galatians 6:2) and hold each other accountable in a loving, restorative way?

   _____

   _____

   _____

   _____

   _____

3. The book mentions the importance of "soul keeping". Let's go around and answer this question: "How is it with your soul?"

_____

_____

_____

_____

_____

- **Action Step:**

  - **Practice Mutual Care:** End the meeting by breaking into smaller groups (2-3 people) to share one specific area where you need prayer and support. Pray for one another. Commit to checking in with your prayer partner once during the week with a simple text: "Praying for you. How are you doing?" This builds the muscle of authentic "siblingship".